The Gospel Flies by Night

Gerhard Padderatz

Originally published in German. This edition published in 2010

Copyright © 2010 The Stanborough Press Ltd.

All rights reserved. No part of this publication may be reproduced
in any form without prior permission from the publisher.
British Library Cataloguing in Publication Data. A catalogue
record for this book is available from the British Library.

ISBN 978-1-904685-63-0

Published by The Stanborough Press, Grantham, Lincolnshire.
Designed by Abigail Murphy. Printed in Thailand.

Unless otherwise indicated, Bible verses have been taken from
the New International Version of the Bible (Hodder and Stoughton).
Other version used, indicated by initials:
KJV = King James Version
NASB = New American Standard Bible (Holman)
NKJV = New King James Version (Thomas Nelson)

Contents

Foreword

As humans, we find ourselves in an awkward position, and that is – we exist. 'Awkward' because, for starters, we had no real choice in our existence. We just one day, as small children, developed a sense of self-consciousness. It comes gradually, imperceptibly really and, before we knew it, we were here, as individual human beings.

All of which leads to the 'awkward' part. Not only did we not choose to exist, we now are confronted with the questions, 'OK, now that I am here, what next?' 'Why am I here?' 'What purpose does my life have?' 'How should I live?' 'What is my destiny?' All things considered, these are not unreasonable questions, and most of us have thought about them at one time or another.

In this book, *The Gospel Flies by Night*, German writer and businessman Gerhard Padderatz explores some of these, the most basic of questions. Basic because, after all, pretty much everything in this world has a purpose, the purpose for which it was intended. One could, I suppose, buy a blow dryer and use it to warm one's food, but it wouldn't be the best use of the product, would it? It wouldn't be fulfilling the purpose for which it was created. Well, if it's that way for a blow dryer, how much more so for human life? How are we supposed to live if we don't know what our purpose is?

Thus, Gerhard Padderitz, on a night flight from the United States to Frankfurt, meets a woman on an aeroplane, whom he calls Margot Naumann – and all night long they explore these questions. It's a dialogue.

A dialogue allows us, in a sense, to be voyeurs. We can listen in over the shoulders of Mr Padderatz and Mrs Naumann as they talk about everything from UFOs to hell, from 3-D movies in Heaven to the vexing problem of human suffering and woe. Whether you agree with Mrs Naumann's scepticism and dismiss Mr Padderatz's faith, or vice versa, it doesn't matter. What matters is that you'll come away from their all-night conversation enriched. And though certainly not solving all of life's grand questions, *The Gospel Flies by Night*, I believe, can provide a framework to help us work through some of the awkwardness of life, a life we've all been given and yet that doesn't come with immediate and overly apparently instructions on how to get the best use out of it.

Clifford Goldstein
Silver Spring, MD

Introduction

We live in the information age. Our home computers carry more facts than most people could acquire in a lifetime of learning. Through the Internet, more information is at our fingertips than is found in the greatest libraries of the world. With the tap of a few keys and a click or two of a mouse, we can have the details that, a generation ago, might have taken weeks, months, or even longer, to find.

No question, we have lots of information, as never before. But how much *knowledge* have we gained? How much *wisdom*? Despite all this information, most people seem to have no answers to the really important questions.

Who are we? Why are we here? What do our lives mean? Does God exist? And, if so, why does he allow so much suffering, especially if he is loving, kind and omnipotent? Should he be trusted or feared? Does he get personally involved in this world or our individual lives, or is he far off, distant, uninterested in what happens here? What happens after death? What is the eventual fate of the world?

These are the truly important questions. They may not help me earn a living, but the answers will have a decisive influence on my enjoyment of life, my inner peace, my emotional health and my interaction with other people. In short, they will have an impact on how I live now.

In Western societies, many people live as if God doesn't exist, or, if he does, it doesn't matter one way or another. Others, open to the idea of the Creator, have too many unanswered questions about him, or they reject the idea of God because they do not understand his actions, or because they see him as unjust or even cruel.

Though I can hardly claim to have all the answers to these questions, I do believe that sensible people can, through the study of the Bible, come to know enough about God, his character and his plans for the world to enable them to come away with good reasons for having faith and trust in the God of the Bible.

Over the years I have grown to appreciate not only the Bible but also each dialogue I have had with others about God. Their manifold objections to God, or to my viewpoints, have helped me to have a better understanding of the complexities and challenges of faith. As a Christian and a management consultant, I am interested in people and their ideas about God, the Bible and faith. On my many job-related trips, I often engage co-travellers in conversations. In most cases it doesn't take long before these topics arise. I have found that when I express my faith in God others become curious, and fascinating dialogues often follow. Most people in Western Europe – and to some degree the sceptical elite in America – consider an educated and professing Christian to be somewhat eccentric.

The following dialogue, which forms the basis of this book, took place on an overnight flight across the Atlantic. Though unable to reconstruct it verbatim, I have managed to bring together the essence of the thoughts. Then, with the help of others, including Clifford Goldstein (who contributed some valuable explanations and arguments and who also polished my English), I wrote this book.

Of course, one could ask, 'Why should anyone have any interest in a conversation between two Germans on an aeroplane?' Fair enough question. The answer is simple: it's because the conversation dealt with questions about the most basic issues of life, those that concern all human beings, regardless of how much or little they consciously think about them.

Though I'm not naïve enough to believe that anyone reading this book will come around to my opinion on each point, my desire is that those who read will be stimulated enough to study for themselves those matters that have important consequences for all of us, regardless of who or where we are.

Gerhard Padderatz

CHAPTER ONE

A Travel Acquaintance

'Are you flying all the way through to Frankfurt, or are you getting off before?'

The lady, already in her seat, looked at me quizzically as I took mine beside her.

'Getting off before?' she asked incredulously. 'There aren't any stops between here and there!'

'True,' I replied as I sat down. 'I should have been worried otherwise, because I can see that you haven't brought your parachute today.'

She burst out laughing. That response, and the fact that she then quickly folded the newspaper on her lap, led me to assume that my co-passenger was open to conversation. On flights, especially long ones, I like to talk with anyone willing to converse, because I'm interested in people's perspectives on the important questions of life and death and God and so forth. I also like to share my own views, and with a non-stop flight from Pittsburgh to Frankfurt we were going to have plenty of time to talk. Eight hours, in fact.

She was, I guessed, in her early sixties. From her diction and mannerisms, I took her to be well-educated and affluent. Her hair was done very nicely and her clothes suggested class and wealth. Just the look in her eyes told me she was bright.

I learnt from my neighbour that she was widowed and had a grown-up son. She lived in Düsseldorf but had a sister in Pittsburgh, whom she had been visiting for a while, and now she was heading home.

'I see,' I said, pointing to her German newspaper, 'that you're catching up with the news from Germany.'

'Yes,' she replied. 'This is today's paper, but it doesn't have anything new in it. Besides, most news is bad anyway.'

'Well,' I said, 'that's how the media works. "Bad news is good news," as the Americans say, which means bad news sells better than good news.'

'It's funny, isn't it,' she replied, 'that most of us want to read bad news rather than good.'

'Why do you think this is so?'

'Perhaps we want to compare the tragedies in other people's lives with our own so we'll feel better. Compared to the many sad stories we read about, most of us are pretty well off, don't you think?'

'Yes,' I said, 'that's true. Most of us are pretty well off, but I don't think that will last. I think the world's getting worse, don't you?'

'In what sense?' she asked. 'Morally, economically or in regard to the environment?'

'In general. Where is this world heading? What will the future bring? What must the whole race brace itself for?'

She then looked at me strangely and said, 'I hope you don't want to talk to me now about religion.' She wasn't hostile but she was firm. 'Please, I don't believe in God.'

I liked her straightforward manner.

'No, I don't believe in God,' she said again, as if more for herself than for me. Then, after a pause, she looked right at me and said, 'But I do believe in guardian angels.'

'Guardian angels! Really?'

'Yes,' she answered firmly, resolutely.

'Why do you believe in guardian angels?' I asked, sensing an opening.

'Oh, I could tell you several stories.'

'I should be fascinated to hear them.'

'When I was 19,' she began, 'my parents, my sister and I had a bad car accident. It was winter and the roads were icy. My father lost control of the car on a curve. We slid off the road and crashed down a slope. We turned over twice. The car was a wreck, but except for a few scratches and bruises, none of us had any serious injuries. We didn't know how we all came through so unscathed. I believe a guardian angel protected us.'

'Very interesting,' I said.

'Another concerns my uncle. His daughter had just had her first baby. When he came to visit her at the hospital, he had a massive heart attack, a man in his early fifties. He sat by her bedside and just dropped to the floor. Because it happened there, they were able, of course, to help him immediately. Had it been anywhere else, he most likely would have died. I don't think it was a coincidence. That's why I believe that each one of us has a guardian angel.'

'I'm convinced you're right.'

'Really, you are?'

'Yes, because the Bible in numerous places talks about the ministry of angels. In the original languages, the word for *angel* reads *messenger*.'

'Really?'

'Yes, and there is more – much more.'

The woman looked at me in anticipation, as if hungry and eager to hear more. I could sense that she was a seeker.

That's why I dared to keep inquiring.

Little did we know that that would go on all night.

CHAPTER TWO

Why Many People Reject God

Someone who believed in guardian angels but not in God. That was a new one. I wanted to pursue this further.

'Tell me; you believe in guardian angels, but not in God. Is that correct?'

She turned to me. To make it easier for her to answer my question, I added: 'I assume you have good reasons.'

She thought for a moment before speaking. And when she did, her words came out fast and full of conviction, with even a hint of anger.

'I was raised in a Christian home. As a child I had to take Bible classes. But there are issues in the Christian faith that really bother me or that I don't understand. I mean, if God really were merciful and powerful, why would he allow so much suffering? Take the simplest example – the sufferings of children, whether in war or sickness or whatever. Why doesn't God intervene?

'That's just one example. I mean, why did God plant the tree of knowledge in Paradise and forbid Adam and Eve to eat from it? And why did he punish them when they did?

'And then there's the Christian doctrine of hell. That always seems so barbaric to me. How can I believe that God is loving and kind when he tortures people in hellfire? When I was a child I lived in abject fear of hell. It was horrible!

'And there's something else. Why do scoundrels and so many bad folk do so well in this world when often good people don't? There's no justice here – none. Shouldn't a just and fair God do something about that as well?'

Then she looked me in the face and, almost accusingly, asked,

'Do *you* believe in a just and merciful God? I am sorry, but I cannot. Our fate seems to make no difference to him.'

I sensed her bitterness, her anger, her pain. I understood it, too, for many people have those same questions. Indeed, I would have felt the same way had I not learned the things I have learned about God and what he is really like.

'Well,' I said, gently. 'You have raised some important questions which have kept me on my toes for quite some time.'

'I have?'

'Of course. Anyone who believes in God wrestles with these issues. The good news is, though, that I have thought about them a lot and have found some helpful answers in the Scriptures. Together with some logical conclusions or deductions, they help me better understand God and the answers to life's difficult questions. I think your questions are good, valid and important.'

'I hope you won't be offended if I remain sceptical.'

'Of course not. I like to hold conversations with people who defend their own points of view. Truth has its own power of conviction. If you're interested, I should like to talk with you about some Bible statements and my thoughts on them.'

'If you promise not to bend my ear too much,' she said, 'because there is one thing I cannot stand – people who want to proselytise others. I am a sceptic and I don't like to be talked to death. You are probably one of those who have found their faith once and for all, and who now seize every opportunity to pass on their conviction to everybody around them.'

She stiffened and her look was feisty and determined. 'Right?' she said.

I smiled at her and explained: 'I should much rather subject my own conclusions to the thoughts of others, because it has always been I who benefited from their objections and questions.'

'If you're looking for objections and questions, then you're talking to the right person; I can promise you that.'

'No problem. Besides, when it comes to objections and questions about God, you're not the only one.'

She looked at me inquiringly. That for me was the sign to continue.

'I once met a theology professor in California,' I began, 'who took his students through all the sixty-six books of Scripture. He always asked the same question: "What picture does each book of the Bible give us about God?" To gather material to illustrate his lectures, he once flew to England, taking a camera team with him. He interviewed many people, always asking them the same questions. The first one was: "Do you believe in God?" Many answered: "When I was a child I believed in God, but I can't anymore." '

'When I was a child I believed, too,' she said. 'But that was probably because back then I didn't know as much as I do today.'

I nodded in acknowledgment of her comment, and continued. 'The professor then asked: "What would a God have to be like in order for you to trust him?" Most of the answers were: "He would have to be like a good friend on whom I could rely." "Someone who would be there when I needed him." "He should understand me and love me and be patient with me." '

'That sounds like a God I could believe in,' she said.

'Good. Well, here's the interesting thing. All those individuals described God the same way Jesus Christ represented him to us, and the way he really is! The God, however, whom they rejected was not the true God but a poor caricature of him.'

'Not so fast,' she replied. 'Those people must have had their reasons for arriving at the picture they had of him. They probably had bad experiences with God. Just look at all the misery on our planet! Where in the world is your God?'

Good questions. How could I answer them?

CHAPTER THREE

The Problem Started in Heaven

Lucifer's rebellion and God's reaction

'The whole matter involves the angels,' I said. 'The angels in whom you believe. Did you know that there was a rebellion in Heaven among them?'

'Really?' she answered. 'The angels?'

'Yes. The Scriptures tell us that there was a leading angel whose name was, according to the Latin translation, "Lucifer". It means "carrier of light" or "the shining one".[1] He was exceedingly beautiful and very intelligent. Lucifer, most likely, was the highest angel at the throne of God – a created being but still perfect.[2] At some point, however, his beauty and intelligence went to his head. The Bible tells us that because of his beauty he rebelled against God.'[3]

'How did that happen?' she said, looking somewhat incredulous.

'The Bible doesn't tell us.'

'No?'

'No, but there is an illustration which has helped me to understand the issue better. How does one find out if one is beautiful? Isn't it in most cases by looking in the mirror and comparing oneself with others?'

'OK.'

'Lucifer must have done something similar. By' – and I created quotation marks with my fingers – ' "looking in the mirror", he must have become aware of what excellent qualities he had compared with the other angels. But looking into the mirror, or to oneself, has one major disadvantage.'

'What do you mean?'

'Lucifer lost sight of God, his Creator, the One to whom he owed everything, even his existence.'

I paused and looked at my companion. I could see that she was listening intently, and so I continued: 'And here is where I find a deep and basic truth: If we lose sight of God, something always goes wrong, at least in the long run. I have seen that happen many times, and have experienced it in my own life, too.'

'Really?'

'Yes. And that was exactly what happened in Lucifer's case. At some point he was no longer satisfied with his position under God. It's hard to understand why. After all, he was the highest created being in existence. The Bible talks about his intention to become equal with God and to rule over the angels.[4] Haven't we come across plenty of that: selfishness and hunger for power? No matter what people have, if they take their eyes off God, it's never enough. They want more. All of that had its origins here, in Lucifer.'

'Unfortunately, that's a widespread problem.'

'We see it all the time. Selfishness was at the root of all evil in the universe. For a selfish person, everything revolves in circles around him- or herself – and these circles keep getting smaller and smaller. This is contrary to God's principle of life – the principle of selfless love. In his case, the circles get wider and wider, in order to include everybody else.'

'OK, but even if what you say is true, why didn't God stop Lucifer's selfish ambitions right away? He's all-powerful, right? Why didn't he just zap him right there and then?'

'That is the all-important question,' I said. 'Let's look at it a bit more closely. First, let me ask you this: What could God have done, what would he have had to do, to be absolutely sure that none of his creatures would ever rebel against him?'

'He would have had to create them perfect, without any bad inclinations at all.'

'Good. Yet, according to the Bible, God had done precisely that. Lucifer is described expressly as the "model of perfection" and "blameless".[5] God created the angels with no defects at all. They were all perfect. But, most importantly, he created them free; that is, he gave them a free will. And that's the reason why they were able to rebel.'

I paused, watching her expression.

My neighbour was in deep thought. She looked at me for a while in silence, and then slowly said, 'I believe I understand where you're heading. He would have had to create all beings without a free will. Only that way could he have been sure that nobody would rebel against him.'

'Exactly. All created beings would have to function like robots or puppets, which leads us to the next important question: If God is God, then he must have known beforehand what would be the result of giving all his higher beings a free will. If so, why did he do so?'

'That's a very good question,' she said, almost angrily. 'If there is a God, that's exactly what I should like to ask him.'

'Fair enough. Let's pursue this further. God created us humans "in his own image",[6] with reasoning powers and the ability to know him. Let's use our reason here and see where it leads us.'

'OK,' she said.

'What do you appreciate most about inter-human relationships?'

She thought for a moment. 'That I can trust someone, and that he or she trusts me as well.'

'Good. And I agree, though I would add that what I value even more is to be loved by someone else.'

'You're right, of course. Love is the most valuable thing.'

'May I ask you a personal question? What would it mean to you, as a mother, if there were a button on the side of your son's head, say, just behind his ear, and each time you pressed it he would automatically say, "Mother, you are the best. Mother, I love you!"? How much value would you find in those words?'

'None,' she said coldly.

'Of course. Without free choice there can be no genuine love. If I had a gun in my hand and waved it threateningly before your face, I could force you to do a number of things, but the one thing that I certainly could not make you do is to love me or to trust me, right?'

'Definitely not.'

'And what I am saying here is that even God cannot force love. Love, in order to be love, can only be given voluntarily. To force love is to destroy it. Even God can't force love.'

She laughed and then said, 'Yes, with a gun pointed at me I should say to your face what you wanted to hear, but the very moment the gun was gone I would look down on you in disgust because it was all a lie. That's certainly not love.'

'Right. For God it was more important that his relationship with his created beings be based on trust and love, and not on the kind of absolute security that comes from force.'

'Security? What do you mean?'

'I mean security from a rebellion against his rule. God could have made sure that there was no possibility of a rebellion simply by not giving created beings free will. Instead, he created a universe in which he allowed the kind of freedom needed for love and trust to exist. But that always brings with it a risk. Yet it is exactly such a God whom I greatly respect and admire, a God who is taking this risk so that there may be loving and trusting relationships.'

'Well, yes, I could agree with you on that one, at least hypothetically.'

'Good. Then let's continue to trace the story of this rebellion. How do you think God might have responded to Lucifer's activities?'

'How should I know? *You* are the Bible expert. So what did he do?'

'The Bible doesn't tell us, at least not directly. In many places, however, God is identified as merciful, gracious and patient.[7] In one biblical account, when he appeared to Moses, he even described himself that way.[8] And because God does not change his character,[9] we can conclude that he reacted to Lucifer the same way – with mercy, grace and patience. He probably explained to him that there was no reason for his dissatisfaction and his striving for more power, and that it was impossible for a created being, in principle, to be equal to his creator. God, I truly believe, would have offered him forgiveness if he had given up his dangerous ambitions and remained loyal to him. Can you imagine how Lucifer might have responded?'

'No, but things are now beginning to get exciting. If I were to put myself in Lucifer's shoes, I probably would try to test God's patience even more and find out how far I could go.'

'That's what children often do with their parents,' I said. 'And if you give in, then they often take that for weakness, and have a greater incentive to continue. That's probably what Lucifer saw in God's gentle reaction – a sign of weakness. In any case, he was determined to assume God's place and position. That much we know, and we know that he drew quite a large number of angels to his side in the rebellion.'

'But why didn't God crush that rebellion at the beginning? Why didn't he kill Lucifer and his followers once he knew that they would not cease their machinations?'

Flies by Night
The Gospel
Flies by Night
The Gospel

'Good question, a very good question. And it leads us to the all-decisive issue that we must investigate. For here is the key to a better understanding of why there is so much suffering and misery in this world, even though God is a God of love. The Bible does not answer this question directly, but it mentions some of Satan's character traits and behavioural patterns that allow us to see what was happening. From that, we can then come to an answer.'

'Satan? Where did he come from? Or I guess that this is another name for Lucifer?'

'Precisely. Through his rebellion "Lucifer", the "carrier of light", of his own accord changed into "Satan". This Hebrew word in its English translation means *opponent* or *enemy*, and it describes his attitude towards God. In the New Testament he is mostly called *the devil*. This word comes from the Greek *diabolos*, which means *slanderer*. We call something diabolic if we mean that it is devilish or satanic.'

'Amazing what's in those names. I never expected that.'

'Christ once called Satan "the father of lies",[10] I continued. 'Today we should say "the mother of all lies" or "the inventor of lying". That's why we can conclude that from the very beginning of his rebellion he was not open and honest, but worked with lies, insinuations and slander. Even when talking to the first human beings he claimed they would not die if they were to eat from the "tree of knowledge", despite the fact that God had said the opposite.'[11]

'Interesting,' she said.

'Now, in order to understand God's reaction to Satan's rebellion better, let me ask this question: How do we get rid of someone who is spreading lies and slander about us? Let me pick an absurd example. Let's say I spread lies and slander about you in Düsseldorf among people who know you. I am sure you wouldn't tolerate that for too long. Let's further assume that, fed up, you shoot me. Bang, bang – dead. What conclusion would the people draw about the things I had said about you?'

'You're right; your illustration is absurd, but for argument's sake, I believe my neighbours, in the first place, would be shocked by my reaction. Only after that would they think about the content of your statements.'

'Of course. They would not have expected that of you. But after a while wouldn't they think: "Hmmm. . . . There had to be some truth in what he was saying because, well, look at her reaction"?'

'That might very well be the case.'

'Therefore, precisely *because* of your violent reaction, my lies would have gained some credibility. Thus, lies cannot be eradicated by simply killing the liar. In the same way, the problem that had arisen because of Satan's lies and slander could not be solved through power and force. In fact, it probably would have made the problem worse.'

'I see your point.'

'Additionally, we learn in Scripture that Satan works with cunning and craftiness.[12] He always presents himself as the good guy. Paul writes that he disguises himself as an "angel of light",[13] which means that he appears as one with good intentions and goals. So, in all his slander against God, he appeared to the angels as their benefactor and tried to trick them into believing that under his government they would be better off than under God's rule.

'Even more so, I think that it was hard for the angels to see through his deception when Lucifer first started his rebellion. They had not known anything like it before. How do you think they would have reacted?'

'Are we in school now? You're addressing me like an elementary school teacher!'

'I apologise,' I quickly replied. 'That's not my intention. By asking you questions, I am only trying to encourage you to give your viewpoint; that's all, as Socrates did in ancient Greece. By asking questions and probing, we both learn. I neither want to sermonise nor to present you with the final answers. Neither would help you in better understanding God.'

'I understand,' she said, sounding calmer. 'Keep going.'

'OK. The question I asked you has helped me a great deal in better understanding an important aspect regarding faith in God. When Lucifer said something that differed from what God had said, the angels had to decide whom they should trust. Now, trust in God was one of the foundations of a perfect universe. The need to believe in God, meaning "to trust in him", existed even for the angels in Heaven, who were able to see God and talk to him face to face. The fact that we must trust in God has nothing to do with the fact that we cannot see him.'

'You said, "*must* trust". But the word "must" doesn't sound much like free choice!'

'You're right,' I replied. ' "Must" really does sound like force. But that's not how I meant it. I meant it more as, well, a necessary precondition. Without trust, harmony could no longer exist.'

'That makes sense.'

'In order to understand God's reaction to Satan's activities, we have to keep in mind something else. What would have been the effect on the loyal angels and all the other intelligent beings if God had just eliminated Satan?'

'He probably would have spared himself a lot of trouble,' the lady replied, 'had he just wiped him out.'

'Maybe. But why don't we call the matter by its rightful name? God would have appeared like a murderer. Someone acts in a way God doesn't like and so what does he do? He just kills him. If he had done so, what would have been the consequence?'

'Most likely nobody would have dared rebel again. The angels would have, I'm sure, become afraid.'

'Exactly. We see something like this in the training of children. Obedience – forced by pressure and intimidation – in the long run produces a rebel.'

'I know how that is. I was brought up with a lot of pressure. It produced fear but no conviction. I know what I'm talking about. Sooner or later one becomes defiant and rebellious – if one is not broken on the inside before then.'

'Yes,' I said, nodding, 'that's right. If God had destroyed Lucifer, the angels would have served him out of fear rather than love, and the germ for the next rebellion would already have been seeded. Satan's lies and slander would have found fertile ground. Therefore, by just zapping Satan, God would not have solved the problem!'

She nodded slightly.

'Now you can answer your initial question yourself about why God with all his power and might didn't eliminate Satan.'

'If he had eliminated Satan,' she said, 'he truly would not have gained anything. Eventually the angels would no longer have felt like keeping up the charade of a faked love, and more discontent could have started again. That is exactly what happens to people who live under dictatorships. It would have been as if God had poured oil onto the fire.'

'That's a very important point. Glad that you see it. The problem caused by Lucifer could not be solved through the use of force. Force would only have made the devil's charges seem true.

'But let's go back again. God had not created a devil but a perfect angel by the name of Lucifer. He was the highest of all cherubim.[14] I'm sure you remember Christmas songs which mention cherubim, the highest angelic beings. It was Lucifer, one of those cherubim, who turned himself into Satan, an enemy of God.

'And so evil had appeared on the scene. What was God to do in order to get it out of this world – or better, out of the universe? How could he convince all the angels and all the other intelligent beings that Satan's claims and accusations were nothing but lies and slander?'

My neighbour looked at me for a while, deep in thought. Then she said: 'Actually, God would have had to conduct a public court trial. Everything would have to follow the procedures of an open and free court case. The evidence would have to be presented, witnesses to be heard, and pleas to be entered. And at the end the jury and some judge would have to come up with a verdict. He who has nothing to hide should not be afraid of a trial – especially not if the court were in a position to bring into the open every hidden fact.'

'This is precisely God's solution to the problem,' I said, not trying to hide my excitement at how she was following my logic so closely that she was actually getting ahead of me. 'In the end there will be a thorough and extensive court trial. But before this can happen, pieces of clear evidence first have to be gathered so that the verdict will be absolutely clear. Otherwise, one claim would simply stand vis-à-vis another claim. You know that from movies with court trials.'

'Right.'

'This means, then, that of necessity God has to give Satan the opportunity to prove his accusations against him and to allow him, by his own actions, to reveal his true character. God can count on Lucifer pulling the mask off his face himself.'

'What accusations?'

'That God is selfish, motivated by a hunger for power and that he is unjust. God only wants to be served by his creatures but won't really do anything for them. The proof to the contrary became evident in the way that God demonstrated his character and principles of government by not destroying Satan right away but responding in mercy and love. Next, he appealed to the judgement of the angels and all other intelligent beings, including humans.'

'That makes sense.'

'Yes, the terrible consequences of Satan's insurrection and his kind of government will eventually become clear before the entire universe. His true character, just like God's true character, will be revealed. Then, in the final judgement, all intelligent beings will be able to form their own picture and come to a just and sustainable verdict.'

'That sounds good,' my companion said.

'In order to have a better understanding of God's actions, there's another important issue to be considered. Because one of Satan's accusations was that God is unjust and unfair – that he will favour some and disfavour others – he has to be absolutely fair towards Satan. Therefore, God must not assume any rights for himself which he is not willing to grant to Satan as well. He must not totally restrict Satan's actions! And that is why he cannot, or I should say *must* not, from case to case remove or hinder their consequences.'

'Does that mean he has to allow Satan to do his thing?'

'In principle, yes. The drama of sin must be played all the way through so that, in the end, everybody will see where rebellion against God leads. All must realise that God really is merciful, loving and just and deserving of our love and trust. That's the only way to make sure that free beings never rebel again. The whole thing works like immunisation. After all questions are answered, and the sin bacillus has produced enough antibodies, the universe will be immunised against any new rebellion.'[15]

'That sounds pretty fantastic.'

'Yes. But I trust that, with this method, God will accomplish his goal. And in a way I am even grateful that it was Satan who started that rebellion.'

'Why is that?' she asked in surprise.

'Because he was the highest created being, and so nobody will ever come up with the idea that he was too dim-witted to see the rebellion through to a successful end.'

'All this is pretty costly, isn't it, just to make sure that the whole thing will not happen again?'

'The price is high, I admit. Higher than you can even imagine now. But after Lucifer had started his rebellion, God could not have acted in any other way if he didn't want to risk losing the allegiance of all his intelligent creatures.'

She looked at me, deep in thought. After a little while she asked me: 'When did this rebellion supposedly happen?'

'The Bible doesn't tell us. However, it must have happened some time before the fall of our ancestors, Adam and Eve.'

'I still have some questions in regard to that.'

'I remember you said that.'

At that very moment dinner was served.

'I am sure a little break will do us good now,' I said.

'I think so too. By the way, I am Margot Naumann,'[16] my neighbour said as she offered me her hand.

I apologised for not having introduced myself earlier, and I gave her my name. Then we ate our pasta in silence.

Notes:
[1] Isaiah 14:12, Vulgate Bible.
[2] Ezekiel 28:14-16, 12b.
[3] Ezekiel 28:17.
[4] Isaiah 14:13, 14.
[5] Ezekiel 28:12b, 15.
[6] Genesis 1:27.
[7] Psalms 86:15; 103:8.
[8] Exodus 34:6.
[9] Hebrews 1:12; James 1:17.
[10] John 8:44.
[11] Genesis 3:4, 5; compare chapter 2:17.
[12] Acts 13:10.
[13] 2 Corinthians 11:14.
[14] Ezekiel 28:14.
[15] Nahum 1:8, 9.
[16] Not her real name.

CHAPTER FOUR

Are UFOs for Real?

Deceptions caused by Satan's angels

We flew into the night. The sky had turned pale orange. For a while we were looking out of the window. Below us was Newfoundland.

'What I always find fascinating about flying,' I said to Mrs Naumann, 'is the fact that above the clouds, at least during daytime, the sun always shines – no matter how grey the sky was at departure. Sometimes I remind myself of that when, on gloomy days, I feel depressed. The sun is shining, I tell myself, even if I don't see it. For me that is a good picture of God's love and closeness.'

'Yes, above the clouds it's always nice,' the lady said while deep in thought. 'And so many things look so small and insignificant from up here. Look, over there, that light. It looks like a UFO.'

She smiled and pointed to a plane with white blinking lights, which was illuminated by the last rays of the sun. It flew next to us but at a safe distance away.

'What's your opinion of UFOs?' she asked all of a sudden. 'Flying saucers – are they for real? Could they be visitors from other planets? Or are UFOs just figments of our imagination?'

'Just a few weeks ago I watched a programme on the state of the research on this subject,' I told her. 'It seems that even serious scientists are now convinced that some of the UFO sightings are not just imagined.'

'But aren't there always natural explanations for those phenomena? In one case it may be the northern lights, in another, a satellite or a hot-air balloon or the like?'

'A major percentage of the sightings can be explained naturally. But some cannot be explained through science, it seems. There are well-documented cases, where pilots, scientists or police have seen objects that seem not to fit into our world-view. They have even examined clear impressions and burn marks in the ground, which apparently were caused by unidentified flying objects.'

'That means you, too, believe there are intelligent beings – aliens in outer space?'

'Yes, intelligent beings, but not in the sense of Martians or what you see in science fiction movies. I believe that some UFO sightings are not figments of our imagination but that those visitors indeed come from another world. According to the Bible, even the angels, in a way, are from outer space. They are aliens of some sort. But they do not depend on spacecraft to get here. They can be invisible or take on a visible form.'

'But if they don't depend on any spacecraft, where is the connection to the UFO phenomenon?'

She wrinkled her forehead.

'Perhaps they are the angels-cum-demons who joined Satan,' I explained. 'Just like the loyal angels, they have special skills and capabilities. They can do things which we cannot explain.'

'I don't understand. If the evil angels can make themselves invisible and don't need any technical help, why in the world should they come to us in UFOs?'

'The Scriptures show us that these evil forces have a great interest in deceiving and misleading us, to turn us away from God and, eventually, to destroy us.[1] That's why I can imagine that demons are behind the UFO phenomena.'

She looked at me in doubt.

'When I was a child – I must have been 12 or 13 years old,' I told her, 'my parents were friendly with an elderly gentleman. His name was Arfst Newton Arfsten and he lived on the North Sea island of Foehr. They always spent time with him when we were on vacation there. When he was younger he had worked as a professor of nuclear physics in Kiel, by the Baltic Sea, and also in New York City. He was a very down-to-earth scientist. In New York he somehow got involved with spiritualism and telepathy. For him those things were nothing but tricks, figments of imagination – just humbug, really.'

'The way I see it, too,' Mrs Naumann interjected.

'That's why he set out to catch his friends red-handed,' I continued. 'In order to uncover their tricks, he participated in some of their sessions.'

'Sessions? What do you mean?'

'You know, the kinds of gatherings at which those present get in contact with the assumed spirits of the dead and communicate with them.'

'Yes, I've heard about that. Aren't those the souls of the deceased?'

'No, most certainly not,' I replied. 'I should like to give you the reason for my opinion later on, in connection with Adam and Eve. The Bible shows us that those supposed appearances of the dead are really demons at work.'

'OK, I'll accept your word for the time being,' she said, somewhat unwillingly. 'So what was it that this nuclear physicist with this difficult name experienced?'

'In one case, the table around which a handful of men had gathered started to move, writing down a message with one of the legs to which a pen had been tied. Our friend assured us that, to his own surprise, no human manipulation had been possible. Another time, a figure appeared out of nowhere and claimed to be the deceased uncle of one of those present. They asked him questions and he gave answers that only the deceased person and the relative present could have supplied.'

'And what did the nuclear professor have to say about that?' she asked, moving to the edge of her seat.

'His world-view was changed by those experiences, to such an extent that from then on he was convinced about the reality of the supernatural, and about beings from outside this world and beyond.'

'But what did he have to do with UFOs?'

'Mr Arfsten once told us a UFO story. It was about an encounter with an alien. A young man in Sweden had witnessed a UFO landing. He was taken into the space ship but then lost consciousness. When he woke up, he found himself in the middle of some sort of spiritualistic session – in Canada!'

'Canada? How could that be?' Mrs Naumann asked, looking at me in disbelief.

'I cannot explain it, but the story seemed credible because I knew Mr Arfsten. I am definitely not surprised about the connection between the UFO phenomenon and spiritualism. Because demons can assume different shapes and forms, it is easy for them to deceive us, make us see things that we think are UFOs and the like.

Their cruellest trick, however, is to appear in the form of deceased loved ones. Satan thus is reconfirming his old lie – the one he had told Eve in Eden thousands of years ago – that despite disobedience towards God, humans in and of themselves possess immortality.'

She looked puzzled.

'This death story you must explain to me in more detail. You had promised that you would come back to it.'

'I'll be happy to.'

Notes:
[1] 2 Thessalonians 2:9, 10.

CHAPTER FIVE

Earth, Breath and Soul

Man's creation

'In the creation story we're told about man's nature,' I explained. 'It says that God formed man "of the dust of the ground".[1] This means that the elements we consist of all exist in the ground but God put them in a special order. How the structure of many vital protein molecules could have originated, even to the present day, is a riddle to science. The Bible then says that God breathed into man "the breath of life".'[2]

'Which means,' she responded, 'that he gave him a soul, right?'

'Not quite,' I said emphatically. 'God breathed into man the breath of life "and man *became* a living soul".'[3]

'That's what I said. He has a soul.'

'But that's not what I said. This is one place where the exact wording in the Scriptures is very important. The Bible does not say that man *received* a soul but that he "*became* a living soul". In the Bible the entire person is called a "soul", a crucial distinction from the common understanding of this topic. In the old days they used to say: "There are 200 souls living in that town," and meant just plain human beings.'

'OK,' she said, showing deeper interest. 'Keep going.'

'The concept that man *consists* of body and soul, and that the soul, after death, will leave the body and go on living forever comes from Egyptian mythology and Greek philosophy. The Bible doesn't mention anything to that effect. Though many people, even Christians, believe that it does, it really doesn't. It's totally alien to biblical thought.'

'But what about the breath? Isn't that another word for soul?'

'Not really. "Breath" *causes* life. That's why it's called "the breath

of life". That's the life force which makes the difference between a "living soul" and a "dead soul".'

She looked confused.

'Perhaps the best way to explain this breath,' I said, 'is by comparing it to electrical power. It was only through this power that the body which God had created became alive.'

'And what does that have to do with death?'

'When a person dies, he or she really is dead – not just without breath but also without consciousness. That person no longer has any part in what's happening here on Earth. This is what the Bible really teaches, despite common notions to the contrary.[4] And that's why the dead can neither appear to us nor communicate with us, which is the precise reason why I'm so sure that evil spirits are behind these spiritualistic phenomena. They want to make us believe that the deceased are not really dead.'

'But then are all those people wrong who believe that the souls of the dead rise into Heaven?' she asked, somewhat bewildered.

'Well, to be honest, they're wrong,' I replied. 'This doctrine of the immortal soul entered Christian thought only *after* the Bible had already been written.'

'I am touched by your faith in the Bible,' she said with biting irony. 'But how do you picture, in a practical way, this idea that God made man out of soil? Come on. How can anyone still believe that, at least with all the knowledge we have nowadays?'

'Well,' I said calmly, 'the biblical account uses only human expressions and illustrations. What else could it use, if we were ever to be able to understand it? But in its essential statements about man's creation, it really does agree with science.'

'Really?'

'Yes.'

'Well, I'm curious to see how you are going to convince me about that one,' she said with a heavy layer of sarcasm. 'Go ahead!'

'Well, for starters, because the story of creation was written more than 3,000 years ago, it naturally does not use today's scientific expressions.'

'That makes sense.'

'Good. Now, when God formed the first human being with "dust from the ground",[5] it meant that he used pre-existing elements and that he brought them into a new, higher order. To use modern terminology, he put information into the matter.

'You see, scientists have quite extensively researched our genes. The quantity of information stored in each gene is enormous. It is far greater than the volume of data contained in a twenty-four-volume *Encyclopaedia Britannica*. That's each single genome! God managed to store all of that in the DNA molecules of our chromosomes.'

'So?' she interjected provocatively.

'So modern information science, which has been developed in connection with computer technology, teaches that neither matter nor time can bring about information. It is true that information is always somehow stored on material carriers, like letters on the pages of a newspaper or a book, or magnetic signals on videotapes, or in digital form on DVDs. But only information can bring about information. Neither matter nor time alone can do that. They need something else.'

She looked at me intently.

'I should like to illustrate my point,' I said, 'with two examples. On a beach, waves will create a pattern in the sand, but they will never write a word – no matter how long we wait. On the other hand, if we find a message in a bottle lying on the beach we are sure – and rightly so – that someone with intelligence has written that message. It did not develop because the bottle had drifted in the water for a long time, right?'

She nodded slightly but reluctantly.

'Anyway, when we put an ape in front of a computer long enough he will every now and then hit one of the keys in such a way that a real word or even a short sentence will be formed. But he will never write a scientific treatise or a novel – no matter how long we let him sit in front of that computer. If we read something profound, we're sure that someone with intelligence has written it, and not the ape.'

'OK, fair enough. But what does that have to do with the biblical story?'

'Evolutionary theory, as commonly understood today, claims that all living beings, including humans, have developed from inanimate matter over billions of years. The theory says that matter and an abundance of time have brought about this enormous amount of information. But, according to information science, that is impossible, because only information can bring about information, and the source of information must contain more information than it can pass on.

'What this means, then, is that the volume of information contained in the chromosomes can in no way have come into existence by coincidence or by chance. One scientist has calculated that the probability of that happening is far smaller than if someone blew up an old-fashioned print shop and the letters in the rubble fell to the ground and, on their own, created a complete dictionary without a single mistake in the type.[6]

'Now, here's the basic point. If a great volume of information is stored in man's genes, then the only logical conclusion is that the source from which it originated must contain even more information. And, because such a source creates a person through this information, logic alone teaches that this source must be greater than the person himself; it must be greater than what it itself created. Such a being, greater than a person, must possess more information than we individual humans do, and we call this being, by definition, God.

'And that's exactly what the Bible says: God brought such an order into common matter – the elements found in soil – that a human body came into existence. And to that body he then granted the power of life, and that's how we or any living thing became alive.'

During my explanation, she no longer looked defiant but startled.

'Does this surprise you?' I asked.

'It sounds reasonable,' she remarked briefly. 'And how did the story of man continue, according to the Bible?'

'Very good question,' I responded. 'Let me explain.'

Notes:
[1] Genesis 2:7, KJV.
[2] Ibid.
[3] Ibid, emphasis supplied.
[4] Ecclesiastes 9:5, 6.
[5] Genesis 2:7, NASB.
[6] Professor Edwin Conklin, eminent biologist at Princeton University.

CHAPTER SIX

A Prohibition in Paradise

Man's freedom and death

'God created a garden, a paradise in which the human beings were to live. They were supposed to multiply and turn the entire earth into such a paradise.'

'Wasn't there also the tree of knowledge from which man was not to eat? I never understood why they were told not to eat from it. Wasn't that a restriction of their freedom?'

'It seems that way, at least at first glance. But a lot more was involved. The answer to that question is very important in order to understand God and the misery in which we humans find ourselves today.'

'OK, explain it to me then – at least your understanding of it.'

'Well, first of all, the Scriptures talked about many trees with all sorts of delicious fruit which Adam and Eve were allowed to eat at their own discretion.[1] In the middle of the garden there was the "tree of life".[2] Its fruit served the purpose of keeping them from getting old and contracting disease. It was rather like the fountain of youth, or something like that. Adam and Eve had to eat from that tree in order to live forever. Only from the "tree of knowledge" were they not allowed to eat.[3]

'The fruit from both of those trees probably looked pretty much the same, and must have been very appealing. Therefore, on what basis were the first human beings supposed to act?'

'What do you mean?'

'When your mother used to say to you, "Do this, but don't do that!" what was she expecting of you?'

'Obedience.'

'Yes, but based on what?'

'Trust?'

'Exactly! And that's the way it was with the first human beings. They, too, were supposed to act on the basis of their trust in God, a trust that led to obedience. Trust was necessary, even though they saw God and were able to communicate directly with him. But God did not coerce them. They were free to choose what they wanted to do.'

'But that's a strange kind of freedom,' my companion protested. 'When I use it, I shall be punished with death!'

'Not quite. It's more like the freedom I have to jump off a high-rise building. When I arrive at the bottom, I die. Is that a punishment?'

'That's a strange analogy!'

'Let me try another, then. You probably had to teach your son not to touch the hot burner on the stove.'

'Well, certainly. Otherwise, he would have burned himself.'

'How did you teach him that?'

'I told him that I would slap him if he didn't obey.'

'Why?'

'Because he didn't yet understand what it meant to burn his fingers.'

'What's the difference between telling him, "If you touch the burner, you will burn yourself" or "If you touch the burner, you will be slapped"?'

'One is a mere announcement, the other a threat.'

'What are you saying with the first one, the mere announcement?'

'What's going to happen if he disobeys?'

'Right, so it is a *consequence* of an act, or, to be more precise, a consequence that you could not keep from happening, unless you were always quick enough to catch your son's hand within inches of the burner each time he reached for it.'

'I'm sure I couldn't have managed that.'

'So, in one case you announce an inevitable consequence, in another an arbitrary punishment. I say arbitrary because you could, if you wanted, choose not to follow through with your punishment.'

'OK.'

'OK; now to which of these would we compare God's announcement when he warned Adam and Eve that they would die if they ate from the tree of knowledge?'

'Where are you heading?'

'We assume that God has given life to man,' I explained. 'He is the source of life and maintains it through the "breath of life", which he first breathed into us.[4] But what happens when we turn away from God?'

'I still don't understand where you are heading.'

'When at night you turn off the light in a room, what remains behind?'

'Darkness.'

'Is there a switch for darkness in your house?'

'Of course not. I have only a light switch, not a "darkness" one.'

'So, when the light goes off, only darkness remains. What happens when we separate ourselves from the source of life?'

'Death,' she replied slowly.

'Yes. Just as when we move away from light there is darkness, when we move away from life there is death. And even God cannot change that, because life is only in him, and so when we move away from him, life, we face death. So God did not threaten Adam and Eve with an arbitrary punishment. Instead, he announced the inevitable consequence that even he himself could not prevent from happening.'

'Yes, he could have,' she protested. 'He didn't have to place the tree of knowledge in the middle of Paradise, did he? And, besides, they didn't know what death meant.'

'Well, let me ask you this: Did your little son at first know what it meant to burn his fingers?'

'Of course not. But he later found out the painful way, I might add.'

'On what basis was your son, then, supposed to do what you told him to do?'

'He was to trust me.'

'Had you given him any reason to mistrust you?'

'I made an effort to avoid that.'

'In the same way, God certainly had given Adam and Eve no reason to mistrust him either. On the other hand, he had given them many reasons to love him. And if I love someone, I like to do what pleases him or her, or what he or she asks me to do, right?'

'But wouldn't it have been safer if there had been no tree of knowledge at all?' Mrs Naumann asked.

'Of course. But what was God up to? Did he, with this tree, only want to annoy or test our first parents? Or do you think that more might have been involved?'

'Spit it out.'

'Yes, but you can figure it out somewhat for yourself when you take into consideration the greater picture, which is the controversy between God and Satan that we have already talked about. If you remember, we had determined two points. First, all the angels in Heaven had to choose whether they wanted to trust God and remain faithful to him or not. Second, God had to remain fair, even towards Satan. That, by necessity, led to consequences regarding how God had to deal with all his intelligent creatures, that is, if he wanted to remain fair and just.'

'You mean that they all had to be able to choose whether they wanted to remain faithful to him?'

'Exactly.'

'So the tree of knowledge was a kind of test to find out which side Adam and Eve would choose?'

'Yes. But it was also a matter of fairness and justice towards Satan that humans had the option to decide whether they wanted to stay on God's side or join Satan. That's what God's prohibition about eating from the tree of knowledge was all about – allowing Adam and Eve to make a choice on whose side they wanted to be.'

'Quite clever, I must admit,' she said, looking satisfied. 'I never heard of that in my Bible classes in school. That's really too bad because it makes sense, at least somewhat.'

'But God also had something else in mind when he did that.'

'There's more?'

'Oh, yes, more than you realise. Through that tree he constantly reminded the first humans that he, God, was the owner of the garden and of the entire earth, and that they would be only his managers, his stewards.[5] Everything belonged to God, nothing to them. That's how he wanted to make them conscious of the limits placed on them and, thus, make sure they wouldn't become selfish. Selfishness, after all, was at the heart of Satan's rebellion to begin with; remember?'

'Yes, I can see your point.'

'And there is still something else. Even though Adam and Eve had been created with perfect inclinations, they had not as yet fully developed characters. In order for character to be formed, we must make moral choices. We are talking about decisions that go beyond choosing a pear or a banana for breakfast. We're talking about choices between good and evil, between right and wrong, that kind of thing.

'With the tree of knowledge God gave them the possibility of making such choices. Over time they would have grown in character – without sinning – until evil would no longer pose any attraction for them at all.'

'That really would have been possible?'

'Certainly. On the one hand it was necessary that man should be put to the test, as were all the other intelligent beings in the universe. On the other hand, this tree also had some essential positive functions for them.'

'I am not sure I have as yet fully understood this thing with the moral decisions,' she said hesitatingly.

After quickly searching for an illustration, I said, 'Let's go back to your son.'

'OK.'

'How old is he?'

'Thirty-nine. Why?'

'Let's assume that we can turn back time and your son is only 6 years old. You love him very much and don't want him to get into bad company and become a drug addict and so forth, and so you don't let him leave the house until he is 25 years old. You teach him at home, you keep him from having any contact with kids his own age, and you make sure that he never watches TV. What will happen when, at the age of 25, he is released into the real world?'

'He will be absolutely unprepared for life.'

'Of course. And wouldn't the danger that he would end up making wrong choices be much greater simply because he had never learned to make moral decisions and how to tell the difference between good and evil to begin with?'

'Yes, for sure.'

'And wouldn't he accuse you of having manipulated him and of being a tyrant because you had never given him the opportunity to choose freely? Couldn't your relatives and the juvenile court system have made the same accusation?'

'They probably would have taken him away from me.'

'Yes. Now let's get back to Eden. God had really made it as easy as possible for the first human beings. Very easy, in fact. I mean, there were numerous trees in the garden from which they could have eaten at any time, and to their hearts' delight. I should have loved to try some of the delicious fruit God provided in Paradise. Sometimes I get a glimpse of that when I eat sun-ripened fruit in Mediterranean countries. Adam and Eve were not in any way dependent on the fruit from the tree of knowledge as they were on the fruit from the tree of life, from which they had to eat in order to stay alive.'

'But I don't understand why, out of all trees, it was the tree of knowledge that was forbidden to them. Knowledge is something good, isn't it? Didn't God want man to learn and become wiser?'

'Yes, he did. But it was not about knowledge in general but a very special kind of knowledge. Not all knowledge is good; wouldn't you agree? How much knowledge should, say, a 6-year-old child have about sex? Remember, the tree in Scripture is always referred to as "the tree of the knowledge of good and *evil*".[6]

'In the Bible, knowledge always has something to do with experience. By eating that fruit Adam and Eve would not have gained additional knowledge, but instead they would have experienced in their own bodies not just good but evil. God wanted to spare them that experience. He never intended humans to know and experience evil.'

'But apparently he did not succeed.'

'Unfortunately not. But that's the risk involved in giving creatures freedom. Satan through Eve succeeded in seducing man to eat from the tree.'

'How was he able to do that?'

'The Bible tells us that a serpent or snake started talking to Eve at the tree of knowledge. He asked her whether God had forbidden them to eat from all the trees in the garden.'[7]

'Oh, yes, the snake, I mean the *talking* snake! Isn't that clear proof the Bible is full of fairy tales? A talking snake? Come on!'

'Yes, I admit, that's strange. Here, though, we come to an important juncture. We either reject the Bible as untrustworthy because of the strange things in it, or we dig a little deeper, apply our minds, and discover important truths that might not seem apparent on the surface. What would you prefer to do now?'

'Stupid question. I think you should know by now that I am a seeker.'

'I apologise. Maybe I didn't word it correctly. I wanted to ask whether we should continue or whether you would rather take a break or sleep a little.'

'Sleep? No way. You've really got my adrenaline going. I'm wide awake. But I could use a drink of water.'

Just as she said that, a flight attendant passed by with a tray of water and orange juice. We both reached for a cup.

Notes:
[1] Genesis 2:16.
[2] Genesis 2:9.
[3] Genesis 2:17.
[4] Psalms 33:6; 104:29.
[5] Genesis 2:15.
[6] Genesis 2:9, 17 (emphasis supplied).
[7] Genesis 3:1.

CHAPTER SEVEN

The Failed Test

The Fall and its consequences

'Well, go right ahead,' she said, resuming the conversation. 'I'm curious what you're going to turn this fairy tale into next.'

'Well, I'm sure that, with a few hints, you will be able to arrive at the most important truths yourself.'

'Go right ahead. Let's see whether you can teach an old dog new tricks.'

'OK, let's begin. It is obvious that Satan had seduced Eve,'[1] I said. 'But where do you think he was in this story?'

'Probably in the snake.'

'Good. If so, then what had he done?'

'Disguised or camouflaged himself?'

'Right. Or, perhaps, we could also say that he used an agent or medium. And so then this serpent was speaking. What does that mean, then?'

'It means that you're telling me a fairy tale.'

'But if it really had happened?'

'Then it would have been a miracle.'

'Exactly. And what did Satan want to accomplish by speaking through the serpent?'

'I don't know. What did the snake say?'

'Well, let's read the passage for ourselves. When I travel I always carry my pocket Bible with me. One moment, please.'

I took the Bible out of my briefcase in the overhead compartment and opened it to the first pages.

'Here it is. In Genesis 3 the Bible tells us the story. "The serpent . . . said to the woman, 'Has God indeed said, "You shall not eat of every tree of the garden"?' " You see, earlier on God had said to

Adam, "Of every tree of the garden you may freely eat."[2] So what did Satan sow by saying that?'

'Doubt and confusion, obviously. God said one thing; Satan, another.'

'Good, very good. So even back then Satan used the same tactic he still uses today. First of all, he never appears personally but always uses an agent, in most cases another person. Secondly, he works miracles to get our attention. The so-called appearances of the dead in séances and other occult experiences are cases in point. Thirdly, he throws doubt on the Word of God and sows mistrust. And fourthly, it is always his goal to seduce us into disobeying God's commandments and to draw us to his side. If we look at it this way, this little story, your "fairy tale", holds some very important truths for us today.'

'That does sound plausible, I have to admit.'

'We can also read how Satan seduced Eve into sinning: "Then the serpent said to the woman, 'You will not surely die. For God knows that in the day you eat of it your eyes will be opened, and you will be like God, knowing good and evil.' "[3] Aren't those enticing promises: immortality, greater knowledge, and to be like God? Doesn't the last thing sound familiar to you?'

'What do you mean?'

'I told you earlier that Lucifer wanted to be like God. Now he tries to get humans to fall into the same trap.'

'Apparently quite successfully, too.'

'Yes, unfortunately. Now we come to an important point. In this version of the Bible, God's statement and the serpent's statement appear right next to each other in two columns. God says, "When you eat . . . you will surely die"; the serpent, however, says, "You will not surely die."[4] A lie couldn't be any more blatant, could it? But sometimes the boldest lies are the most effective.'

'When it came to lying, my husband was a champion,' my companion said, grinning. 'But let's go back to Eve, the victim and the perpetrator.'

'Yes. What decision was she facing?'

'To determine who was right.'

'And how could she have found out?'

'Try it out and see, I suppose. But that was her doom, wasn't it?'

'Yes. That was the very thing she was not supposed to do. So, first of all, she was facing the question of whom she should trust – God or the serpent. Again, trust plays a major role.'

'Fair enough.'

'Good. So what exactly was Eve's sin then?'

She thought about it for a while: 'It was a breach of trust towards God – and it was also selfishness. But then Eve did not die right away, did she? Wasn't Satan partially right after all?'

'Let's see. Look at the serpent's promises once again. In what way was he right?'

Mrs Naumann once again read the verses in my Bible. 'Oh, yes, the knowledge of evil – or the experience of it, as you called it.'

'So what was Satan's strategy?'

'He mixed truth and lies.'

'And that's what he is doing up to the present day – and very successfully too.'

'I am beginning to understand why you find the Bible such an interesting book.'

'Oh, there's plenty more in here, believe me. But let's take a closer look at this. Let's look at Adam's role now. He, at first, is not mentioned here at all. He appeared afterwards when he saw Eve with the bitten fruit in her hand. He probably soon realised what that meant: he would lose her. What a decision Adam was facing then! Should he eat from the fruit as well? If not, he would lose Eve; if he ate, he would lose God but die with Eve.'

'Poor Adam!' my neighbour said with a smile. 'His love for Eve put him in a tight spot.'

'Right. But wasn't it on a deeper level a matter of love in the first place? Whom did Adam love more: God or Eve? Of course, it's right to love one's spouse, but you probably know "the greatest commandment" as Jesus called it.'

'What commandment was that again?'

'To love God with all your heart, with all your soul and all your strength.[5] This is the greatest commandment. That's where Adam sinned. He showed a lack of love towards God, which was why he disobeyed in the first place. Interestingly enough, whom do you think the New Testament blames for all the misery in the world today? Who, in your opinion, carries the greater responsibility for all this?'

'Well, ultimately the snake, but then . . . Eve, perhaps?'

'No, it was Adam. He was not seduced; Eve was.[6] Instead, he sinned willingly, and with eyes fully open too. The actual sin of the first human beings, therefore, consisted in lack of trust and lack of love towards God. You might have experienced for yourself, or surely you have been a witness to the effects of a serious breach of trust or love in a marriage.'

'Oh, yes, many marriages have broken up precisely because of that.'

'Has it become clear now how by this "fall", as it is commonly called, the relationship between man and God was destroyed at its foundation?'

'No, not really.'

'OK, look at it like this. After a serious confrontation or fight between people, someone sometimes says, "This person is dead to me." The Bible talks about a "spiritual death", when a person has no relationship with God. In that sense Adam and Eve had died right away; in a physical sense they died later on. And, as a result of their actions, we find ourselves in this situation, that of a broken relationship with God. Their fall impacted the whole human race. We feel the results of it today, each one of us.'

'But what would have happened if Adam and Eve had not eaten from the tree? If they hadn't, would they not then have made use of the freedom God gave them?'

'Well, I would look at it like this: they would have used their freedom of choice to trust in God and not to eat from the tree of knowledge. They had the freedom to choose either way. If they had used their free choice to obey, then we should be living in Paradise today. And there would be no mistrust, no war, no disease and no death. All the while our freedom of choice would have remained intact.'

She stared at me intently.

'Let's take a closer look at the consequences,' I said, taking advantage of her keen interest. 'The Bible tells us that Adam and Eve were hiding from God when he came to visit them in Paradise.[7] Fear had replaced love. And when he addressed them in regard to their transgression, Adam blamed Eve, and then she went ahead and openly blamed the serpent. Look at how Adam phrased it: "The woman *you* gave to be with me," he said to God.[8] So whom did Adam actually blame?'

'God.'

'Isn't that typical! We blame God for the bad things we have done ourselves.'

'I don't, because I don't believe in God.'

I had to ponder my response carefully. 'OK,' I said, 'but I often hear many people who don't believe in God sometimes say when disaster strikes: "Why didn't God stop this from happening?" '

She didn't respond.

'Anyway, let's return to the first sin. There was, then, suddenly, discord between Adam and Eve. Thus, we can see that because of their disobedience their characters and their relationship with each other had been affected. Their disobedience also meant the end of their lives in Paradise. Work from then on would cause sweat and toil. Pain and disease appeared as well.[9] Humans also faced death, something they were never intended to experience. I am sure you know God's statement to them, for it's often quoted at funerals: "For dust you are and to dust you will return." '[10]

Mrs Naumann nodded her head.

'So Adam and Eve were driven from Paradise because they were unfaithful managers. They were denied any further access to the tree of life.[11] That actually was an act of mercy on the part of God because, otherwise, there would have been immortal sinners.'[12]

'So what?'

'So what? Let me ask you, Would you like to live forever under the conditions we have in this world today? Imagine being in this mess *forever!* How much would you like that?'

My neighbour wrinkled her forehead. Then she got up, fumbled in her handbag and sat down again with a pack of paper tissues in her hand, and gently wiped her face.

Notes:
[1] Revelation 12:9.
[2] Genesis 2:16, NKJV.
[3] Genesis 3:4, 5, NKJV.
[4] Genesis 2:17; 3:4.
[5] Mark 12:29, 30.
[6] Romans 5:14; 1 Timothy 2:14.
[7] Genesis 3:8, 10.
[8] Genesis 3:12, NASB (emphasis supplied).
[9] Genesis 3:16-18.
[10] Genesis 3:19.
[11] Genesis 3:23, 24.
[12] Genesis 3:22b.

CHAPTER EIGHT

Our Second Chance

What makes salvation work

When she had finished, she looked at me defiantly and said: 'Isn't it unfair that we all have to suffer for Adam and Eve's sin, and that because of them – folks I never met – I am mortal?'

I paused to ponder before answering.

'Well,' I began slowly, 'God is the Creator and, therefore, the source of life. Through their disobedience the first human beings separated themselves from God,[1] and thus they cut themselves off from their source of life. Our mortality is a necessary consequence of this separation. After all, Adam and Eve were not able to pass on to their descendants what they did not possess themselves. They no longer had immortality, so how could they pass it on to us? What they did pass on to their children, however, was their inclination towards sinning. That became evident in their son Cain, who out of envy killed his brother Abel.'[2]

'We're really stuck in a mess because of Adam and Eve then, aren't we?' Mrs Naumann said, smiling.

'Yes, but we need to remember that God does not hold us responsible for inherited inclinations. But he does not prevent us from suffering the consequences of the Fall. For he cannot completely do away with the law of cause and effect. Otherwise, we could not trust anything anymore. Life would be impossible.'

'What do you mean?'

'OK, just imagine if, at the airport, God suddenly negated the law of gravity, so that an old lady, in the process of falling down the stairs, would not break her bones. Fine, but the other people would suddenly start floating in the air and the planes couldn't land anymore because gravity would not pull them down to the

ground as usual. Right now, I cannot think of a better example. But I hope you understand why the law of cause and effect is fundamentally important, even if that has negative consequences at times.'

'Yes, I do understand that.'

'God had clearly warned the first human beings of the consequences of disobedience.[3] Had those consequences not come about because God had prevented them, he would have lost credibility. The basis of trust would have received a crack. And, all of a sudden, Satan with his lie, that man would not die, would have been right. Thus we can see the dilemma God would be in if he got rid of the natural consequences of sin.'

'I'll have to think about that in a quiet moment.'

'Fair enough. I know that this is a lot to take in.'

She nodded and then said, 'Please, continue.'

'Well, in connection with these questions, we must never forget the bigger picture: the great controversy between God and Satan. Satan's schemes had to be allowed to play themselves out, in order for the entire universe to see where they would ultimately lead. And, for that to happen, sufficient opportunity had to be provided. Abusing their sacred gift of free choice, the first human beings decided to stand on the side of Satan and, unfortunately, we have all suffered the consequences of their bad choice.'

'Oh, really!'

'But hear me out. God could not prevent those consequences if he wanted to reach his goal, which is one day again to have a universe in which harmony, love and peace rule. To all creatures endowed with reason it had to become clear where rebellion and disobedience, known as sin, would lead.'

'But has that not been clear for quite some time?'

'Yes, at least to the loyal angels. When through human agents Satan made sure that Jesus Christ, the Son of God, would be crucified, he very clearly revealed to the loyal angels his true character: he proved himself to be a murderer, as Jesus had said,[4] even a murderer of God.

'As a consequence, God was able to banish Satan permanently from his presence in Heaven, without casting any doubt in the minds of the loyal angels about his justice. He banished him to the earth because only here had Satan found followers.'[5]

'That sounds pretty strange to me,' she said defiantly.

'I understand; believe me, I do. It took a long time before I saw the connections. We do not know all the facts; that's for sure. Some things we can understand now; others, he will explain to us in court when he is completing his plan of salvation and bringing final closure to the great controversy.'

'One thing I still don't understand: If God is almighty and supposedly so merciful then couldn't he have accomplished our salvation some other way – without Christ having to be crucified first? Couldn't he have sent an angel or simply said, "Let's forget about the whole thing. I will forgive you everything. Nobody will be lost"? Why did his Son have to die to put everything in order again?'

'Your question is fully justified. I have talked to many people who don't understand God's actions in the plan of salvation. Until recently I myself did not understand it so clearly. But then a friend sent me an outline he uses in his Bible studies and it helped me greatly. Are you interested?'

'Yes, I am. I can't sleep anyway,' she said, leaning back in her seat.

'My friend argues that God's proceedings in connection with our salvation follow, by necessity, from the consequences of the initial sin. We've already talked about those consequences. The consequences and at the same time the cause of our calamity are lack of trust and lack of love towards God. Mistrust and selfishness replaced them. What, then, did God have to do to motivate man to trust and love him?'

'Well,' she said hesitatingly, 'I guess he would have to demonstrate that he could be trusted after all and that he was worthy of our love. Somehow he had to repair the relationship.'

'Yes, but God cannot restore the relationship to man all by himself. Both sides have to work on it. He can only show his interest in a harmonious relationship and *prove* to us his trustworthiness and love. It is not enough for him just to *claim* that he is trustworthy and lovable.

'At the same time, he has to give Satan the opportunity to prove his claims and thus give man the chance to identify them as lies. (Satan must be given enough rope to hang himself. His true character is being exposed, a character dominated by selfishness, greed, love of power, and bloodthirstiness.)

'Another consequence of sin is that, consciously or unconsciously, we have joined Satan's rebellion and have become disobedient towards God. We ignore his commandments. What, then, can God do to change that?'

My neighbour looked puzzled and then said, 'He has to make man turn away from Satan – or what?'

'That's right! God has to motivate us to give up our rejection of him and to separate ourselves from Satan. In other words, he has to take us to the point where we obey him out of love.'

'Obey out of love?' she asked. 'But that doesn't go together. Isn't obedience something compulsory, the opposite of freedom and love? If I love a person and that person loves me too, then I don't talk about obedience.'

'You're right. If I love someone I shall do everything possible not to spoil my relationship with that person. I shall try to live and act in such a way that there will be harmony, for us to be of one accord in regard to interests, goals and values.

'On the other hand, we must never forget that God is the Ruler of the universe and that there is order in his Kingdom. We call this order the law of God. I am sure you know the Ten Commandments.'

'Of course I do.'

'After all, they are given to us for our own good, our own best interest. They protect us – our lives, our property and our marriages. That's why they read, "You shall not murder, steal or commit adultery." These commandments come from a loving and wise Creator who knows how to make us happy. In regard to God, therefore, it is indeed appropriate to talk about obedience.'

'I see.'

'The nature of my relationship with God naturally has a strong influence on what motivates me. I can be afraid of him and obey him because of that. If, however, I love and trust him, then I shall express that love by following his principles and instructions.[6] Jesus once said to his followers, "If you love me, keep my commandments," or, more correctly, "If you love me, you will keep my commandments." And, "You are my friends if you do whatever I command you."[7] Jesus is not our buddy, but the Son of God. As our Saviour, he is always our Lord to whom we listen and whom we follow.'[8]

'I like that better,' my co-passenger said.

'Good. Now let's move on to another consequence of sin,' I said. 'Because of the transgression of God's clear commandment, the first human beings became guilty and deserved punishment. Through our own behaviour today, we pretty much show that we wouldn't have done any better because we, too, frequently and knowingly transgress God's commandments.'

'That's for sure.'

'And thus we suffer from guilt, right? I mean, we all do. So the question is, "What did God have to do to free us from our guilt?" '

'Forgive us . . . ?'

'Forgive a guilty person his just punishment? But that violates our sense of justice, doesn't it? Couldn't Satan in that case accuse God of injustice? And wouldn't he be right in doing so?'

She nodded.

'So, it's not quite so easy, is it? God cannot just sweep our guilt under the carpet. He is indeed merciful, but he must also be just.'

She looked at me and wrinkled her forehead again.

'Man's guilt somehow had to be atoned for and, at the same time, justice had to be served. But in the process God could neither punish man the way he deserved – because that would mean eternal death – nor could he remove or change his commandments, which are the basis of his moral government. What would we think of a God who would first give us commandments and then, when we transgressed them, alter them to meet us in our transgression?'

'We should probably lose respect for him.'

'Right! Also, an additional problem was that man's character, through his disobedience, was changed as well. Man had become selfish and had thus lost his suitability for a life in a perfect universe. What requirements was God facing in regard to this problem?'

'I don't understand.'

'Our character had to be changed without God's manipulating us. That was exactly the challenge: he had to find a way of changing our nature in such a way that we once again lived in harmony with his character and principles. And, in the process, God could neither force nor manipulate us. He needed the willing co-operation and consent of each person.'

'How was that supposed to happen?'

'I'll come to that in a moment. First, we should consider two additional requirements for God. Mankind was subject to physical decay, disease and death. On top of that, Adam also had lost Paradise. What could God do if he wanted to remove all those consequences of the Fall?'

'Well, he had to make man come back to life and he had to create a new Paradise.'

'Exactly. God had to give us a new life in a healthy body and completely re-create the earth. If he would then grant us access to the tree of life, we could live forever.'

'Then everything would be perfect again,' Mrs Naumann said. 'That's a lot for God to do, I'd say.'

'That's for sure. Fortunately, God is a powerful Creator and very wise. For him, I am sure, it's no problem to re-create mankind and give us a new Paradise. After all, he created Paradise once before, and so he can surely do it again simply through his power. Also, to prove his trustworthiness and 'love-worthiness' is not hard for him either, because that's his essential nature. But some of the listed requirements he cannot fulfil merely by the exercise of his divine power.'

'What do you mean?'

'How do you make a rebellious child obey you once again out of love? Do you have a recipe for that?'

'One would have to try it with a lot of love and persuasion,' Mrs Naumann said.

'Would that guarantee success?'

'Unfortunately, not always.'

'But with force you accomplish even less. That way you would only pour oil onto the fire of rebellion, because the use of force creates fear, right?'

'Hmmm. . . . Quite a tricky situation has resulted from the first sin,' she said. 'I'm beginning to understand that even God cannot solve the problem the simple way. How can he solve it, then? I am sure the Bible deals with that issue as well.'

'Certainly. Now, there are things you might still remember from your Bible classes in school, right?'

'I am sorry, but I can hardly remember anything. Are you referring to eternal life?'

'Yes, the faithful ones will rise one day and receive new bodies.[9] And then they will live on an earth made new where there will be no suffering, pain or death.[10] That's one aspect of how God solves all this. The other is the way in which God has atoned for man's guilt, which we discussed earlier on.'

'You're probably referring to the crucifixion of Jesus. I still don't understand why that was necessary.'

'OK, let's look at that a bit more. Suppose that I'm speeding in my car and get caught in a radar trap. A police officer stops me, wants to see my driving licence and insurance, and then I collect a fine. He can't just forgive me the fine, even if he wants to, because that way he will be violating the law himself and neglecting his duties. But if my friend in the passenger seat pays the fine for me, I end up paying nothing – no fine or penalty.'

'That's a strange example.'

'Sure. That doesn't happen often – but it would be legal. In a similar way, the Son of God paid our penalty, the penalty we owed.[11] That way we can legally remain unpunished, for it is a generally recognised principle of law that *two* persons cannot be punished for the same crime or offence if only *one* of them has committed it. In my illustration, the officer cannot demand the fine from me, if my friend has already paid it.'

'I can see that.'

'Let's now come to the question of why only the Son of God himself could pay this penalty. The atonement, to be just, has to match the crime. You cannot atone for murder with a small fine. The transgression of the divine commandments, however, is a capital crime to be punished by the death penalty, the loss of life forever. Even though we don't like to hear that, it is the truth.

'We as humans are placed under the law of God. God has the right to expect obedience to the law from us. That's why the sacrifice of one human being or one angel would not have been enough to atone for the guilt of all men. Only someone who was equal to the law or above it would suffice. That's why the sacrifice of the Son of God was required. He, as the Law-giver,[12] stands *above* the law. His atonement, therefore, is sufficient for *all* men. If an angel or a sinful human being should sacrifice himself – apart from the fact that there is no sinless human being – this sacrifice at the most could benefit only one other human being, no more.'

'I see.'

'Think, too, what this means. No matter who we are, no matter what we have done, because of Jesus we can stand perfect in the sight of God. Our past sins are completely forgiven and Jesus' perfect record of a sinless life is credited to us by faith. There's nothing else we can add to it. The moment we accept Jesus, we stand perfect and forgiven before God. That's why it's called the "good news".'

'Yes, that is good news, isn't it?' My neighbour then yawned. 'I am sorry. This is not an expression of boredom. Do carry on. When I get tired I'll let you know.'

'Please do. After all, we are digging our way through some very difficult questions about God.'

'You can say that again!'

'But we have tackled quite a good number of issues already. A few minutes ago we stated that God had to prove his worthiness of our trust and love. And that's exactly what he has done.'

'I am not really aware of that.'

'God has proven his uniqueness and his trustworthiness most of all through the prophecies and predictions found in the Bible.[13] Many came true in exactly the way they had been foretold. And because of the fact that he liberated Israel from Egyptian bondage and led his people through the desert into the promised land, he demonstrated his love, faithfulness and trustworthiness, for he had promised their ancestor Abraham that he would do that.'[14]

'Wait a minute,' Mrs Naumann interrupted me. 'Did you just say that God made predictions about the future that later on came true? Could you give me some examples?'

'I'll be happy to. But let's finish first what we're doing now, and then we can look at some examples of fulfilled prophecies in the Bible.'

'Agreed.' And with a wily smile, she added, 'But don't you forget it!'

'I promise. Anyway, we were talking about how God had demonstrated his love. He also did that by sending his Son to Earth. I'm sure you know the verse in the Bible where it says, "God loved the world so much that he gave his only begotten Son, so that everyone who believes in him will not be lost but receive eternal life."[15] The Son of God became a human being and lived among us.[16] He demonstrated in his character and in his actions how much God loves us.[17] On our behalf he even gave himself up to be crucified.[18] That's how much he loves us. Even though ultimately it was the devil who killed him, Jesus could have chosen not to let that happen. After all, he is the Son of God and could have called an army of angels to rescue him.'[19]

'But he didn't, of course.'

'No, because then we would have had no way of being saved. As I said, only someone equal to or above the law could have paid on our behalf the penalty for breaking it.'

'I see.'

'Good. That's why nobody, except the Son of God – who had become a human being – could have saved us.'

'OK.'

'God, with his plan, accomplished his goal only because someone became involved as a Mediator. This Mediator had to fulfil certain requirements. Earlier on, we stated that God had to prove himself worthy of our trust and love. He did that most of all through this Mediator who had to represent God's character faithfully, that is, in such a way that we humans could comprehend it. For that to happen, the Mediator had to fulfil two requirements: be equal in nature to God and be one with us as human beings, so that he could communicate effectively with us. That way he also was able to become our substitute and defeat Satan in his realm.'

'Yes. That makes sense.'

'You see, our problems ultimately have their cause in the fact that we have sinned. The Mediator could not have a part in that. As a human being he had to be perfectly obedient and remain without sin. He had to prove that, through the power of God, we as humans could be obedient and live in harmony with the will of God and that Satan could not force us to sin. Thus it was made clear that human beings really do bear the responsibility for their sins with all their consequences.

'Another requirement we've already discussed: the Mediator had to take upon himself the guilt of all men and suffer the punishment for it. Additionally, he had to be able to free us from our bondage to Satan and our sinful habits. So he had to be more powerful than Satan.

'Moreover, he had to be in a position to free us from all the consequences of sin, especially death. That required that he himself had to overcome death by rising from death. And, finally, in order for him to make us humans rise from death and to turn the earth into Paradise once again, he had to have creative powers. So he had to be equal with God.'

'That's a lot.'

'Yes, it sure is. Let me summarise these requirements, because this point is important. First, this Mediator had to be equal to God, but at the same time become a human being.[20] Second, he had to live a sinless life and, through his death, atone for our guilt.[21] And, finally, he had to rise from the dead and have creative power.[22]

'In the entire universe, only one could fulfil all that: the Son of God, who in Jesus Christ became a human being. That's why he's the only one who could be our Saviour and Mediator.'[23]

'And how could I claim this Mediator for myself?'

'Mankind's calamity, as we have seen, started through a disintegration of a trusting and loving relationship with God. This relationship we must rebuild. God, for his part, is doing whatever is necessary to accomplish this. He does not expect us to trust him blindly. If we get to know a person and find him trustworthy, we will have good reason to trust that person. That's why our first and foremost responsibility lies in getting to know Jesus Christ, for through him we also get to know God.[24] The main sources for this are the gospels in the New Testament.

'When we start loving and trusting Jesus we can take the decision to accept him as our Saviour.[25] We confess to him our guilt and hand over to him our case.[26] From that moment on, we stand perfect before God, sinless in his eyes, because Jesus is our substitute. But there's even more.

'Because we are in that situation ourselves, and because our biggest problems are within us, this means that we hand ourselves and our lives over to him. He will then change us from within so that we shall shed our bad habits and live according to his commandments and principles.[27] That, however – as I have already said – will happen out of love, once we really get to know him and have found out how worthy he is of our love.'

She was thinking it through. For a while we didn't say anything.

'All the things you have told me so far sound plausible. But . . . '

'But?' I asked.
'But how do I know that all this is true?'

Notes:
1 Isaiah 59:2.
2 Genesis 4:8.
3 Genesis 2:17.
4 John 8:44.
5 Revelation 12:7-9; John 12:31.
6 1 John 5:3.
7 John 14:15; 15:14, NKJV.
8 Luke 6:46.
9 1 Corinthians 15:21, 22, 42-44, 51-53.
10 Revelation 21:1, 4.
11 Isaiah 53:5, 6.
12 Compare Exodus 20:2 with Jude 4b, 5 and James 4:12 with
    John 5:10, 11.
13 Isaiah 46:9-11; 45:21.
14 Deuteronomy 7:6-8; Genesis 15:13, 14.
15 John 3:16, paraphrased.
16 Philippians 2:5-7.
17 1 John 4:9, 10.
18 Philippians 2:8; John 10:17, 18.
19 Matthew 26:53.
20 John 1:1-4; Philippians 2:5-8.
21 2 Corinthians 5:21; Hebrews 7:26, 27.
22 Revelation 1:18; 21:1, 5; Colossians 1:15, 16.
23 Acts 4:12.
24 John 14:7; 17:3.
25 Acts 16:30, 31.
26 1 John 1:7-9.
27 Ezekiel 36:26, 27.

CHAPTER NINE

Why I Trust the Bible

Examples of biblical prophecy

'The only reliable source of information for these topics is the Bible,' I said.

'You seem to be convinced about the reliability of the Bible, don't you?' she responded.

'Yes, I am.'

'But how can you be so sure? Isn't the Bible just like any other book – written by people, with mistakes and contradictions and so forth?'

'Well, after a thorough examination, I have come to the conviction that God inspired the authors of the Bible to write down certain events, experiences and direct messages from him. But, that being said, it does not mean that he dictated every word to the writers. That explains why there are very different styles, as well as imperfections in representation and expressions in the Scriptures. I believe, however, that the Bible contains information from God, and that its message is reliable.'

'That's what *you* believe! But what proof is there?'

'Quite a bit, actually. I was especially convinced by the prophecies about the future,' I explained. 'God claims to be the only one who can reliably predict future events.[1] The devil or human beings can prophesy the future, but only to the extent that they themselves can influence or manipulate it. And, of course, there are certain scientific laws which allow us to make predictions with some accuracy, predictions about things like the trajectory of a rocket and so forth. But that doesn't make scientists prophets. And it wouldn't be anything special for me to predict that we shall land in Frankfurt either, would it? With great probability that will happen, but my prediction doesn't make me a prophet.'

She looked at me sternly but said nothing, so I continued.

'I promised you some examples of biblical predictions. Because today we can check their fulfilment beyond any doubt, we have a good test for God's trustworthiness, as well as for the supernatural character of the Bible.'

'OK, give me an example.'

'For starters, there's a prophecy about the city of Tyre. In antiquity that city was a blossoming harbour town on the Mediterranean, located in today's Lebanon. Tyre was the hometown of the Phoenicians, whose trade routes took them into the Atlantic. When the Babylonian king Nebuchadnezzar had conquered and destroyed Jerusalem, the people of Tyre planned on taking advantage of the situation.[2] Through the prophet Ezekiel, however, God had informed them that Nebuchadnezzar would destroy their city as well. On top of that, he warned that it would be torn down, its stones thrown into the sea, and that it would never be rebuilt. In fact, it was never again to be found, even if one should look for it. Sometimes I ask myself whether Ezekiel would have written down what he did, with such surety, had he known today's methods in archaeology.'

'Does it state that so clearly?'

'Why don't you read some of the verses yourself?'

I opened my Bible to Ezekiel 26 and said, 'The prediction runs through an entire chapter. I'll show you only the most significant statements.'

I first pointed with my finger to verses 3 and 4 and began reading: ' "Therefore thus says the Lord God: 'Behold, I am against you, O Tyre, and will cause many nations to come up against you, as the sea causes its waves to come up. And they shall destroy the walls of Tyre and break down her towers; I will also scrape her dust from her, and make her like the top of a rock.' " '[3]

I looked up at her.

'After that God mentions Nebuchadnezzar by name and declares how he will conquer the city.' I pointed to the verses 7 to 9: ' "I will bring against Tyre from the north Nebuchadnezzar king of Babylon, king of kings, with horses, with chariots, and with horsemen, and an army with many people. He will slay with the sword your daughter villages in the fields; he will heap up a siege mound against you, build a wall against you, and raise a defence against you. He will direct his battering rams against your walls, and with axes he will break down your towers." '[3]

When I finished that section, I said, 'After this we find a significant change in the prediction from *he* – referring to Nebuchadnezzar – to *they*.' I read verses 12 and 14: ' "They will plunder your riches and pillage your merchandise; they will break down your walls and destroy your pleasant houses; they will lay your stones, your timber, and your soil in the midst of the water. . . . I will make you like the top of a rock; you shall be a place for spreading nets, and you shall never be rebuilt." '[3]

Then I pointed to verse 21: 'Here, at the end, you can read the prediction that they will never find Tyre again: " 'I will bring you to a horrible end and you will be no more. You will be sought, but you will never again be found,' declares the Sovereign Lord." '

'And you're saying that all that came true?'

'Yes, precisely.'

'What happened?'

'A short time after Ezekiel's prophecy, Nebuchadnezzar besieged the city with his army in the year 587BC. The inhabitants were not too concerned because they were able to flee to an island off the coast. That's where the harbour installations were which were effectively protected against enemy battleships by underwater barricades. Besides that, they had with them warehouses with sufficient supplies for a siege. That's why Nebuchadnezzar was able to conquer and destroy the city on the mainland, but not the island. A peace treaty was signed and the city was soon rebuilt.'

'So the prediction didn't come true after all!'

'Not so fast. About 250 years later Alexander the Great came along. On his great worldwide conquest, he passed the city. The inhabitants of Tyre didn't want to surrender and so, as their ancestors had done before, they retreated to the island. The ingenious strategist Alexander, however, thought of a plan. With the rubble from the city of Tyre itself, he built a causeway to the island. It was 600 metres (1,800 ft) long and 60 metres (180 ft) wide. To do that he used all the material from the city of Tyre. Thus, as prophesied by Ezekiel, all the rubble was indeed thrown into the sea. He then captured the island.

'After that, the city was never rebuilt. The island with the causeway was gradually turned into a peninsula. There is a fishing village on it today, where the fishermen hang their nets out to dry. But nobody knows exactly where the old city of Tyre was located on the mainland. Except for parts of a water pipe, which apparently supplied the city, archaeologists have not found any remnants of it.'[4]

'Really?'

'Yes. Everything happened exactly the way God had predicted it.'

'That is, indeed, impressive,' my co-passenger said. 'Do you have more examples?'

'Sure. Long before its golden age, it was prophesied that the city of Babylon would one day not be inhabited anymore, even though it was located in a fertile area on the Euphrates River. It would become nothing but ruins inhabited by desert animals.[5] Babylon continued to exist for several hundred years more but then it was abandoned and buried in the desert sand. For more than a thousand years nobody even knew where the city had been located. It was not until the end of the nineteenth century that archaeologists dug out ruins, which they identified as Babylon. Except for the curator of the museum, nobody lives there today.[6] The desert animals were able to inhabit the excavated ruins. That way God's prediction was fulfilled precisely after more than 2,500 years.'

'But if folks were digging at the site, there must have been people living there,' Mrs Naumann interjected.

'Well, it depends upon how you want to define "live". If you take it in the sense of being inhabited, then, no, no one has "lived" there since antiquity. In fact, in the old location of the city of Babylon no settlement has ever been developed.'

She remained silent, as if in deep contemplation.

'Do you want to hear more?'

'Yes,' she said. 'Please, go ahead.'

'Another remarkable example is the prophecy of Jesus about the beautiful temple in Jerusalem. He foretold that the temple would be destroyed and that not one stone would remain on top of another.[7] In that context, he also warned his followers to flee the city right away when an army besieged Jerusalem.'[8]

'What happened then?'

'The Jewish historian Josephus told about the tragic destruction of the temple by Roman soldiers. That was in the year AD70, a little less than forty years after the prediction of Jesus.

'During the long siege of the city, the army suddenly retreated. Many thought that it was a trick, an ambush, and therefore did not use the opportunity to escape. Those who followed Jesus, however, remembered his words that that was the predicted sign for their escape and they escaped. Not a single one of them was, we believe, killed in connection with the siege of Jerusalem.'

My neighbour was quiet for a while. 'Can I read up on that somewhere?'

'Sure, the prediction by Jesus you can find in the gospels, in Matthew 24 and Luke 21. The fulfilment is described by the historian Flavius Josephus, who was living at that time. It's in his book *The Jewish War*. You can read more about these examples in books about biblical prophecies and about the results of historical research and archaeology.

'By the way, a little less than 300 years later there was an attempt to prove the prediction of Jesus wrong. The Roman emperor Julian wanted to have the temple in Jerusalem rebuilt. Despite the joint effort of the Jews and the Roman emperor, the undertaking failed. The historian Edward Gibbon reports that balls of fire would rise out of the ground and singe the workers.[9] Thus the people were forced to stop the construction work. Even if it didn't happen that way, the fact remains that the temple was never rebuilt. For centuries now in its place stands the Omar mosque, the Dome of the Rock, the second most holy place of Islam. A rebuilding of the temple, therefore, is out of the question. That would trigger a war.'

'Very interesting. . . . Do you have more?'

'The most impressive examples for the fulfilment of biblical prophecy are the ones about Jesus himself. Several of the Old Testament prophets predicted a number of things about the Messiah – the Saviour – centuries before he appeared. There is exact information in regard to his place of birth, his ministry, the circumstances of his death and his resurrection. There are even precise statements about the time when he would appear and die as a sacrifice.[10]

'You probably know that shortly after the birth of Jesus wise men from the east came and presented him with gifts. When they came to Jerusalem, they asked where the newborn king of the Jews was to be found. But there nobody knew about him. King Herod called in the scribes and questioned them. They named Bethlehem as his place of birth because the prophet Micah, 600 years before, had prophesied that the Lord of Israel would come out of Bethlehem.'[11]

'I remember reading that story at Christmas.'

'Of course. The statements by the wise men and the scribes must have been so convincing that Herod later on ordered the killing of all the little boys in Bethlehem because the wise men had not told him – even though he had demanded it – the whereabouts of the child.[12] He had wanted to get rid of a potential rival. Why should Herod have ordered such a cruel and unpopular measure if he had not believed in the reliability of the prophecy?'

Mrs Naumann looked at me.

'By the way,' I continued, 'centuries before, through Isaiah, God also had foretold that the Saviour would be mistreated and killed for our sins. He was to be buried in the tomb of the rich and he would rise again.[13] In Psalms 22, the kind of death was predicted, crucifixion – even though it was not invented until centuries later.'[14]

'When did Isaiah live?'

'In the seventh century before Christ.'

'Couldn't the followers of Jesus have manipulated all that in order to fulfil the predictions?'

'Not really.'

'No?'

'Well, in 1947, a complete copy of the book of Isaiah and fragments of other Old Testament books were found in caves at the Dead Sea. It could be proved that they dated from the second century *before* Christ. They agree with the biblical text that we have today.'

'That's interesting.'

'Besides that, the fulfilment of most of the predictions neither the disciples nor Jesus were able to influence. The Jewish leaders pursued his crucifixion, and the Roman procurator Pontius Pilate ordered it. That is, a lot of things were totally out of their hands.

'One thing especially impresses me: It was even predicted that Jesus would be handed over for thirty silver pieces.[15] The high priests who paid Judas the money would have had to be the most unlikely people in the world to have an interest in adding to the credibility of Jesus of Nazareth and his claim to divinity.'

'It does sound impressive, but . . . '

'But?'

'But I don't think one can prove the correctness of the Bible with arguments from the Bible itself. Isn't that a kind of circular reasoning?'

'You're right. But the existence of Jesus and his crucifixion under Pilate are facts of history.[16] Because essential parts in this puzzle are confirmed by independent sources, I trust the rest of the story, the parts that aren't depicted in other sources.'

'That's plausible.'

'Now, let me ask you a question, if you don't mind.'

'Sure.'

'What conclusions do you think we can draw from these examples of fulfilled predictions?'

She thought about it for a while, then she said carefully, 'It looks as if the Bible really is a special book. If all the things with the prophecies and their fulfilment are correct, as you say, then at the very least it's mysterious. I have no explanation for that. What is your conclusion from these things, though I can already guess?'

'Because only God knows the future, I conclude from these fulfilled predictions that God has revealed himself in the Bible and that he is trustworthy because what he has predicted has come true. That's why I trust him and why I rely on his statements in the Bible.

'And if so many predictions, as we can prove, have already come true, then to me it would seem only logical that the other prophecies will come true as well, the ones which relate to the future.'[17]

'Which ones?'

'The ones about the Second Coming of Christ, the resurrection of the dead, the judgement and the creation of a new and perfect earth in which there will be no suffering and no death. That all of these things will actually happen is, I think, a logical conclusion, given how true and accurate the other predictions were.'

'Why?'

'It's like this. We, standing here today, can look back and see how predictions in the past came true, just as God said that they would. So, if he was right on the things he predicted in the past, things that have already come true, then am I not justified in

expecting that these prophecies concerning the future will come true as well? God was right on all the others, so why should I not trust him on those yet to come?'

She looked at me with great attention.

Notes:
[1] Isaiah 46:9-11.
[2] Ezekiel 26:2.
[3] NKJV.
[4] Siegfried Horn, *Auf den Spüren alter Völker*, Hamburg, Saatkorn-Verlag 1979, p. 239-47.
[5] Isaiah 13:19-22.
[6] Horn 47-53.
[7] Matthew 24:1, 2; Luke 21:5, 6.
[8] Luke 21:20, 21.
[9] In *History of the Decline and Fall of the Roman Empire*, chapter 23.
[10] Micah 5:2; Isaiah 7:14; 9:1, 2; 53:2-12; 61:1-3; Daniel 9:24-27.
[11] Matthew 2:1-6; Micah 5:1, 2.
[12] Matthew 2:8, 12, 16.
[13] Isaiah 53:7, 9.
[14] Psalms 22:17-19.
[15] Zechariah 11:12, 13; Matthew 26:14-16; 27:3-10.
[16] Flavius Josephus, *Antiquities of the Jews*, XVIII, 3.3; Cornelius Tacitus, *Annals* XV, 44.
[17] 2 Peter 1:19-21.

CHAPTER TEN

Can We Love a God of Torture?

The error about hell

'That makes sense,' she said. 'I'll have to ponder this a bit. . . . But there's something else that bothers me.'

'OK,' I said. 'What is that?'

'When I was a child, the concept of a hell really made me afraid. Whenever I got into trouble I thought that I was going to burn in hell for my transgression.'

She laughed, although these thoughts brought her some pain.

'As I said, what you have said so far makes sense. But what kind of God would torture people in hell for all eternity? Can you tell me that?'

'Good question, and I have to agree that this is one reason why many people reject God. After all, how can I love a God who will throw me into a burning fire if I don't obey him and then, on top of that, will use his life-sustaining power to prolong my torment for all eternity? No wonder some people become disgusted with the idea of God. Or they become afraid of him – and understandably so. For we cannot be afraid of God and yet at the same time love him dearly.'[1]

'But doesn't the Bible talk about hell? Won't God judge the world and punish "the lost", as you call them?'

'Well, that's true, but we must understand exactly how that happens in order to prevent us from developing a wrong picture of God. Scripture does talk about an eternal fire that will destroy the devil, demons and all those who will not be saved.[2] But there will definitely not be eternal torment for the lost.'

'Really?'

'Of course not. Who could love a God like that?'

She seemed surprised.

'Look, the Bible says more than once that God himself is a *consuming* fire.[3] That refers to his glory, which for sinful man has the effect of a *destructive* fire. Don't miss that word "destructive".'

'How does that work?'

'God possesses an enormous radiance or glory. Whoever is not in harmony with him will not be able to stand it. That's why the Bible stresses that we as humans cannot bear his immediate presence,[4] even though he longs to be close to us. We would burn up or evaporate in his immediate presence.'

'So we must be afraid of God after all, because he will destroy us, right?'

'Whoever does not have a pure relationship with God will and must be afraid of him. That's the way it also happened with Adam and Eve who, if you remember, were afraid of God after they had sinned.[5] Only love for God can dispel this fear.[6] When we love him we need not be afraid of him because he will and can save us. Whoever has come into harmony with God doesn't have to be afraid of him or fear his glory. Otherwise, on the new earth the saved could not tolerate God's presence. But the Bible says that they will see Christ as he really is.'[7]

'I still have some more questions with regard to the new earth.'

'Sure, but let's first deal with this question about how the lost will perish. It is very important.'

'Yes, please.'

'Now, Jesus announced to his disciples that he would return to Earth in his divine glory.[8] The faithful followers of Jesus alive at that time will be changed, and the dead believers will be resurrected. En masse they will be taken up into Heaven.[9]

'But the others – the ones who do not have a relationship of trust and love with Jesus – will, of necessity, perish because they cannot bear his glory. They will die.

'Look at this analogy. The most powerful source of energy we know is nuclear. We can do a lot of good with it, such as generate electricity and we can power boats and even submarines. On the other hand, if we are exposed to atomic radiation without protection, we shall definitely die. Therefore, when it comes to the death of the lost, we are dealing with the tragic consequences of human sinfulness clashing with God's radiation or glory. And because God is eternal, the Bible talks about eternal fire.'[10]

'So it isn't God, after all, who will intentionally kill people,' Mrs Naumann concluded.

'Yes and no. Sometimes in the past God interfered in human events to make sure that evil people died so that they could no longer have a negative influence on others. That was the case with the Flood, with Sodom and Gomorrah and with some of Israel's enemies.[11] But God will give life back to *everyone*.[12] One day he will awaken everyone, even those who perish at the Second Coming of Christ. But that will not happen until the judgement.'[13]

'And what happens then?'

'Then the final judgement will be held. God will show to all people who have not come into harmony with him how they have rejected his offer of salvation and wherein lies their guilt. In other words, they will know *why* they are lost. When he has given reason for his sentences, he will once again reveal his entire glory. It will then destroy those humans. But this act will not last forever. Only the *consequences* will be forever. All those who have not come into harmony with God will be dead forever.'

'But what about hell?' Mrs Naumann asked. 'Are the . . . what am I supposed to call them?'

'The most appropriate expression probably is "the lost".'

'Are the lost going to hell?'

'There is no hell in the common sense of the word – a place where the lost will be tortured forever. That is a Catholic tradition which has, unfortunately, made its ugly way into Protestant thought as well.'

'Nothing of this sort is mentioned in the Bible?' she said with some scepticism.

'Well, some verses that graphically illustrate the fate of the lost can be misunderstood that way, but when studied in context and with other texts, the meaning becomes clear.[14] The point is that when Paul talked about "everlasting destruction", as in the book of Thessalonians, the *destruction* itself, the consequence, is everlasting, eternal, not the act itself. In Revelation 20, for example, it says, 'Fire came down from heaven and *devoured* them.'[15] This fire, as we have explained before, is God's glory.[16] Because the lost are not in harmony with God, they cannot bear his presence and they die forever. The death is forever, not the act of destroying them.

'Those who have hardened their hearts towards God the most will resist God's glory the most and, therefore, they will suffer longer. It follows, then, that Satan will suffer the longest. But he, too, will eventually be destroyed by God's glory.'

For a while my neighbour was thinking. 'The way you are presenting it, I can accept. It makes so much more sense than the typical idea of this eternal torture. I was just thinking, too. If the lost, as you call them, were tortured forever, then hell would exist parallel to the new Paradise. In that case it would be hard to see how folks could enjoy eternal life on the new earth when, next door, relatives or friends were writhing and moaning and suffering the tortures of hell for all eternity. The whole idea is pretty absurd, isn't it?'

'You're absolutely right. And how does that harmonise with God's loving character? That, for me, is the most convincing argument,' I explained. 'Lately I have become very sceptical towards all explanations or Bible interpretations that put God in a bad light.'

'What I still cannot get out of my mind is the question, "Do I or don't I have to be afraid of God?" ' Mrs Naumann said, looking at me in expectation.

I had to think carefully.

'We certainly don't have to be afraid of God,' I said slowly. 'I think we should fear the *consequences* of what will happen if we don't come into harmony with him before we die. But the good news is that through Christ we can come into harmony with him, and then we shall be able to stand in the presence of God and enjoy eternal life, the eternal life that God had planned to give us from the start.'

Notes:
[1] 1 John 4:18.
[2] Matthew 25:41; Revelation 20:10.
[3] Exodus 24:17; Deuteronomy 4:24; Hebrews 12:29.
[4] Exodus 33:18, 20; 1 Timothy 6:16.
[5] Genesis 3:10.
[6] 1 John 4:18.
[7] 1 John 3:2.
[8] Matthew 16:27; 24:30; 25:31.
[9] John 14:3; Matthew 24:31; 1 Thessalonians 4:15-17.
[10] Isaiah 33:14; Matthew 25:41.
[11] Genesis 7:17-23; Genesis 19:24, 25; Exodus 14:26-28; 2 Kings 19:35.
[12] 1 Corinthians 15:22-24.
[13] John 5:28, 29; 2 Corinthians 5:10.
[14] Matthew 13:41, 42; 25:41, 46; Revelation 20:10.
[15] Revelation 20:9b.
[16] Isaiah 33:14.

CHAPTER ELEVEN

More than Plastic Surgery

The resurrection of the believers

It seemed as if each answer of mine always triggered a new question from her.

'Earlier on you were talking about the resurrection of the dead,' she said. 'How am I supposed to picture that? They will not be just floating around as ghosts, will they?'

'Certainly not. When Jesus met his disciples after his resurrection, he asked them to touch him so that they could see he was truly real, physical, and not some sort of ethereal spirit. He also had a meal with them to prove that he was still a human being of flesh and blood.'[1]

'The way he was before?'

'Yes. Now think about the incredible implications of this; think about the love for us it reveals. When he was born into this world as a baby, he connected himself to us for time and eternity. While he now, as our Mediator, is sitting in Heaven next to the throne of God, he still has his human form.[2] And he will always have it, for all eternity.'

'But I don't understand how the resurrection is supposed to work with us as humans.'

I thought about it for a while, unable to find a suitable illustration. Then I said, 'Some TV programmes offer a complete makeover to women with considerable physical imperfections. The network offers to pay for all the plastic surgery and styling if the ladies agree to have the whole process filmed for their show.'

'Yes, I've heard of that but have never watched it.'

'I watched one of those programmes. The title was "Extreme Makeover". At the end they showed the lady being presented to family and friends. All were moved to tears because of the incredible transformation. The TV audience was able to see her before and after. It was really impressive.

'But this enormous change doesn't even come close to what will happen to Christians at the resurrection. Even though "resurrection" is the common term used, and rightly so when we think of the resurrection of Jesus, in regard to the believers it would seem more appropriate to talk about a new creation, because they really receive from God a totally new body.'[3]

'Will it be similar to the body we have today, or completely different?'

'Paul wrote that we as humans, after the resurrection, will be "conformed to his . . . body",[4] which seems to indicate that our bodies will have certain similarities to what Jesus has. We shall have bodies as perfect as did Adam and Eve in Paradise. And the best part is that whoever was old, sick, fragile and ugly will then be healthy and beautiful and in the prime of life.'

'That's interesting,' she said, looking at me, somewhat incredulous.

'Most of all, we shall be able to embrace many of our loved ones, friends and family members, and celebrate a reunion, for in many ways we shall all be the same persons we were in this life.'

'You're a dreamer,' Mrs Naumann blurted out. 'I am sorry, but I can't believe all this. How could it be possible? When a person has lain in the ground for a few hundred or even thousand years, nothing will be left but a few grams of carbon or dust. He or she will be completely decomposed and all the elements which once made up that person become part of something else – the trees, the dirt, bugs and bacteria. How can someone come back to life and be the same person that he or she once was? That's too much!'

'You are absolutely right.'

'What?'

'From a purely human point of view, you are right. That would be impossible – just as impossible as it was for God to create man in the first place. But he obviously did it; otherwise we wouldn't be here. And if he could create mankind out of unstructured matter, then he also should be able to re-create completely the saved with their bodies and the personalities they had developed during their lifetime. In no way will he depend on the specific ingredients or elements that we as individuals consist of today. After all, which ones should he take? Biologists tell us that our human cells replace themselves every few years, anyway.'

She peered at me, still somewhat sceptical, but I sensed a little softening.

'Look at it this way. Even we humans, with our technical capabilities, can store enormous quantities of data and do a lot with it, too. Just think of Dolly, the cloned sheep. The DNA of a single cell was sufficient to breed an animal that was virtually identical to another one.'

'That's true.'

'And if we can do that, think of what God, the Creator, can do. He can store in his "brain" the necessary data of each and every human being who has ever lived. And as the Creator he will have no problem whatsoever in re-creating each person. Just the information alone is necessary, not the specific material elements. After all, it is a re-creation,[5] not a reawakening of the old material to eternal life.'

She nodded slightly.

'Here's another way to look at it. Have you ever read about all the galaxies in the universe?'

'What do you mean?'

'I mean, have you ever read about how many hundreds of billions of galaxies are out there, with each one containing billions of stars?'

'Yes, it's pretty awe inspiring, isn't it?'

'Now, just a thought. There are more galaxies, *galaxies*, than there are human beings who have ever lived on the earth. And, again, each one of those galaxies has more stars than the number of humans who have ever lived.'

'I think I see where you are going.'

'Yes – the God who could create all these galaxies should be able to handle recreating the relatively paltry number in comparison of human beings who are going to be resurrected. The existence of all those galaxies doesn't prove that he will; it just seems to give powerful empirical evidence that, if he wants to, he can. After all, however hard it is from a human perspective to believe in the resurrection of the dead, it's no harder than understanding how God could have created and now sustains all those billions of galaxies, is it?'

'No,' she said. 'I guess not.'

And with that, we both lapsed into a calm silence. I didn't want to

Flies by Night
The Gospel
Flies by Night
The Gospel

say any more. Rather, I wanted to give her time to think, which she
was obviously doing.

Notes:
[1] Luke 24:39-43.
[2] 1 Timothy 2:5, 6.
[3] 1 Corinthians 15:35, 38.
[4] Philippians 3:21, NKJV.
[5] Revelation 21:5.

CHAPTER TWELVE

The Hilo Tsunami

Christ's Second Coming

'And when is this . . . what am I supposed to call it now?'
'The resurrection?'
'Yes, when is this resurrection supposed to take place?'
'When the Son of God returns to this earth as the King of the universe. He himself announced to his disciples that he would appear as the Son of Man in divine glory. All the people will see him in the sky. The host of the loyal angels will accompany him and alert everyone on Earth through some type of loud noise. The Bible likens it to a trumpet blast.[1] That's why no one on Earth will miss this event.'
'And what will happen then?'
'The people of all ages who have formed a relationship with God will be re-created to eternal life. They will never die again. And the faithful followers of Jesus who are living on Earth when he returns will be instantly transformed into their new bodies.'[2]
'And what about the others?'
'The rest of the dead will remain that way until the second resurrection.[3] And we've already talked about the effect of the glory of the Son of God on those people who have not received him as their Saviour and Lord.'
'Oh, yes, unable to bear Christ's glory, they will die. How pleasant!'
'Like all the dead, they will then be unconscious until the second resurrection.'
'A *second* resurrection? I was barely getting my mind around the idea of the first one. What is the second one now? Will those people have a second chance to make a decision for Christ?'
'No, not at all. According to the Bible, that's not an option.[4] Everybody has the opportunity to put his relationship with God in

order only as long as he or she lives here and now. God gives everyone the chance to do so. That's what the judgement is all about, showing the universe that he gave people opportunities. That's why Jesus called this second resurrection the "resurrection of condemnation" or judgement.[5] All the lost will be present in the final judgement.'

She looked at me for a while, wrinkling her forehead. 'Are you seriously telling me that the world will end like that? A nuclear war – *that* I could imagine. Or the hole in the ozone layer getting so big that we all get zapped by radiation from the sun. That, too, is plausible. But something like the Second Coming of Christ? That sounds too fantastic, like some sort of science fiction movie.'

'I understand. It really is an unusual event, something that has never happened before. But that, in and of itself, is no valid argument. Just because something has not already happened doesn't mean it can't happen in the future, right?'

'Yes, I guess.'

'There is even an example or a type of precursor to which Christ himself pointed: the Flood.[6] God had called Noah to announce that event to the world. But nobody had ever experienced anything like it before – not even close to it.

'The only indication of the coming flood was Noah's preaching about it. Period. Nothing else. It will be the same with the Second Coming of Jesus. Faithful Christians will tell everyone that Jesus and the judgement are coming and they will point all people to the possibility of salvation through Jesus.'

'Like you are doing now, with me.'

'Exactly, now that you mention it.'

'I see.'

'We who live today should find it easier to believe God's message than those people who lived before the Flood, because the Flood really happened, as science is increasingly accepting. And, as we've seen, we have many examples that prove God's predictions do come true.'

'Yes, but the Flood, Noah's ark and all that, this is just another one of those stories that don't sound credible to me.'

'Well, there is an abundance of geological evidence in many parts of the earth that such a flood took place. And flood stories and legends have been found in many, many ancient cultures, stories that resemble the one in the Bible. But in this context I should like to give you a modern example.'

'Go ahead.'

'A few years ago I watched a report on TV about gigantic waves, so-called tsunamis. The word means "big wave in the harbour". The report dealt with the little harbour town of Hilo on one of the Hawaiian islands. Folks had lived in that town without any worry for hundreds of years, because they had never before experienced a tsunami. But suddenly, on 1 April 1946, there was a big wave.

'The only warning they had had was the fact that the ocean at first seemed to run dry. The water had actually moved back and exposed the ocean-bed. The people thought that that was strange but they ran out to gather the fish that were strewn all over the exposed ocean floor. But then, as if coming out of nowhere, a huge wave suddenly arose and swept them away. One hundred and fifty-nine people died. Survivors later reported that the wave had been 30 metres (90 ft) high. It caused great damage and had been triggered by a distant earthquake in the ocean floor.'

'Go on.'

'As a consequence of that catastrophe, the American government installed a tsunami-early-warning system. It included, among other things, sirens which were also set up in Hilo.

'Then in May of 1960 there was a great seaquake off Chile. By then it was possible to predict fairly accurately how many hours later a tsunami would hit Hawaii. The Hilo sirens sounded so that everybody could run to safety. Since their installation the sirens had sounded more than once, but in each case the waves had turned out to be pretty harmless. That was why the people of Hilo had developed the habit of running to the harbour whenever the siren sounded. They wanted to look in amazement at the big waves that were coming in. That's the way it also happened that night in May of 1960.'

'What happened?'

'The first two waves, indeed, were not especially big. The third one, however, was a so-called killer wave. It was supposed to have been more than 10 metres (30 ft) high. Again the town was largely destroyed and many people lost their lives because they were standing on the shore.'

'When something like that happens you have no chance,' Mrs

Naumann mused out loud as she looked down to the floor in bewilderment.

'Well, that's not quite true. One of the workers in the harbour who was interviewed for that TV programme had survived because he had climbed into a boat and sailed into the sea. That was his ark. The boat survived the tsunami because the wave had built up so high only near the shore.'

'Your point?' she asked firmly.

'Just as with the Flood in Noah's day the people of Hilo had been warned. But they could not imagine such a disaster happening to them again. I'm afraid many will be in a similar situation when Christ returns.'

'Perhaps we, too, need some kind of ark.'

'Yes, certainly. In hymns, God's Church is sometimes compared to a ship in which one can be safe. I think that is a beautiful picture. But we must not think that a formal membership in a church will ever save us for the new earth. For that purpose it is necessary that we consciously entrust ourselves to Christ, live with him, trust in his merits, and allow him to change us.'

'Yes. You've already said that.'

'Yes, I have, and that's because I believe it's the key to everything else. Everything.'

Notes:
[1] Matthew 24:30, 31.
[2] 1 Thessalonians 4:16, 17; 1 Corinthians 15:51-53.
[3] Revelation 20:5, 13.
[4] Hebrews 9:26-28.
[5] John 5:29, NKJV.
[6] Matthew 24:37-39.

CHAPTER THIRTEEN

3-D Movies in Heaven

The millennium and God's judgement

For a while we looked at the stars. I sensed the endlessness of space and also the closeness of God. Was she, perhaps, feeling something similar?

'If there really is a Second Coming of Christ,' she suddenly asked, 'what will happen afterwards? And how do you picture eternal life? Eternity is a long time. Isn't that going to be boring?'

'Not at all. According to the Bible, we shall not be bored. We shall be reunited with friends and loved ones, and we'll meet many interesting people and make new friends. We'll use our talents and be productive.[1] We'll do work we enjoy and never get tired.

'Most of all, we shall get to know God the Father, and Jesus Christ.[2] When he explains the plan of salvation and the deeper issues of the controversy with Satan to us, we shall love him even more. I look forward to listening to one of his sermons.'

She looked at me, but with none of the incredulity I sensed earlier, and so I continued.

'Besides that, we shall travel to other planets and visit their inhabitants. We shall be able to talk to them about the events on Earth and about what sin has done.'

'That does sound interesting. A few minutes ago you said that there would be a second resurrection, one connected to the judgement. What's that all about?'

'The judgement is very important for a better understanding of God, because more than anything it will be about vindicating him.'

'God's vindication?' My neighbour wrinkled her forehead again (the incredulity was back).

'Yes. That has something to do with the lies and slander Satan has spread about God. Many people believe them. Even Christians have many questions they would like to ask God. Why he did one thing and not another. Most of all, the saved want to know why some relatives or friends are not with them.'

'That, of course, is a moving question.'

'God will take a lot of time to justify himself and explain his actions. In the Bible that's called "the judgement of God". Yes, in a real sense, God allows himself to be judged by his own creatures. That says a lot about his character, don't you think?

'I should say so.'

'The judgement is really an evaluation of God and his actions; thus the final judgement on his character is still pending. After all, Lucifer has slandered him. Then all evidence will be put on the table and all God's decisions will be reviewed.'

'That's interesting.'

'One thing is for certain: God doesn't need the evidence and the judgement to decide about our salvation. But *we* and the angels need the evidence to gain absolute certainty about God's character and the correctness of his decisions. Does that make sense?'

'Go on, please.'

'OK; now in this three-part trial it will become evident that God, in fact, has acted in love, mercy and righteousness in all cases. Sure, I know that many struggle with this idea. Even I have a lot, and I mean a lot, of questions.'

'You said a three-part judgement. What do you mean?'

'We are talking about three different phases, three different groups. In the first phase of the judgement, God will justify himself before the angels and before Satan in regard to the salvation of the saved.'

'But why is that necessary, before Satan, this, well . . . devil ?' Mrs Naumann asked in consternation.

'It's like this. The devil considers all human beings his property, for *everybody* has followed his principles more than once. Some have rebelled against God or even placed themselves openly on Satan's side. That's why the Bible says that all of us have sinned and are guilty before God, and it's why Satan maintains that if God is just, then by no means can he grant us eternal life. Otherwise, God would have to forgive him, Satan, and his followers as well.'

'Go on.'

'The loyal angels are concerned about another question. Because of the events surrounding the crucifixion of Jesus, they have already seen the result of Satan's rebellion against God and recognised his true motives. Thus they have been confirmed in their loyalty towards God. But they, of course, don't want another rebellion in Heaven, and if God wants to grant eternal life to many people who once rebelled against him, then there is a real danger that this will happen again.'

'I can see that.'

'So God must explain to the angels how he can grant eternal life to human beings without their being a security risk on the new earth or the restored universe.'

'I can imagine that won't be easy.'

'It certainly isn't. For even the saved will continue to have a free will and the power of choice.'

'And how does he manage to fight off Satan's claims and put the faithful angels at peace?'

'This is where Jesus Christ as our substitute and defender plays a decisive role. If, in a way, we have handed over to him our case by accepting him as our Saviour and have confessed to him our trespasses and sins, then he can point out that all Satan is bringing up against us (and correctly so, I might add) is already on record in Heaven. Christ can then claim the merits of his sacrifice in our behalf and point out that, through his suffering and death, he has already paid the penalty for us on the Cross.'

'I see.'

'This leads to something important, too. By saving us, God is going to bring sinners into Heaven, into a perfect environment, even though Satan and his angels are going to be left out. How fair is that?'

'Good question, I suppose.'

'But the fact is that by giving themselves to Jesus, these people have shown their love and their loyalty is to God. Satan hasn't done that. On the contrary, he remains at enmity with God. Thus, God can justly bring these people into Heaven, not because they are worthy but because they have surrendered themselves to the Lord, giving him love and loyalty, something that Satan and his demons won't do and thus they don't belong there.'

'That seems to make sense. OK, but let me ask you now about the other phases of judgement.'

'First, let me add two more sentences to the first phase: It must, of course, happen *before* Christ's Second Coming, because by then the final separation between those who are saved and those who are lost will have happened. A biblical prophecy from the book of Daniel shows us that the first judgement phase has already been in progress since, I believe, the mid-1800s.'

'Really? So we can calculate the end of the world after all?'

'No, by no means, because we do not have any statement about how long this phase of the judgement will last. God has revealed to us something only about the beginning of that judgement. Talking to his disciples, Jesus clearly stated that we cannot find out the time of his Second Coming. Therefore, all speculations are futile.'

'Can you explain to me the prophecy that puts the judgement in the mid-1800s?'

'I can, but I would rather not do so at this time.'

Mrs Naumann looked at me in surprise: 'But why not?'

'Well, this isn't the time and place to study it. Besides, for the issue we are dealing with in this context – the beginning of the judgement – it doesn't play any major role anyway.'

'OK,' she said, 'but you wanted to tell me more about the other two phases of the judgement.'

'Yes, I'll be happy to. The second phase, *after* the Second Coming, will deal with the vindication of God vis-à-vis the saved. They, too, will have a lot of questions, especially about their relatives and friends who are missing. Therefore the cases of all the lost will be reviewed. Christ himself will be the judge, and the saved will be the jurors in this phase of the judgement.[3] That, by the way, is the reason why I am convinced that basically God will subject his sentences to a review.'

'It's kind of sad,' she said, 'that there are so many people among my friends and loved ones who don't believe in God. And most likely I shall be among the lost as well.'

I kept quiet and looked at her. She was fighting her tears. Finally, she took her handkerchief and wiped her face.

'It doesn't have to be that way,' I resumed gently. 'The decision whether or not you will be lost is basically yours. God loves you and wants to save you. You only have to accept his salvation and allow him to work in you.'

'Well, OK, I can still think about that.' She was fighting to regain her composure. Finally, she said, apparently pained, 'And what will happen next to the lost?'

I thought for a while about whether it would make sense to continue with the subject. But because she had asked a specific question, I decided to answer it.

'Have you ever been to an IMAX cinema,' I asked, 'and have you seen a 3-D movie there?'

'Yes, I know what you mean. You have to put on some special glasses and then you are right in the middle of the action.'

'Right. I imagine that God will use something like that to present to us the cases of all who have been lost. We shall be able to see what God has done to reach everyone and cause each person to put his or her relationship with God in order and accept Christ as Saviour. We shall learn, for instance, why some of our relatives, despite God's wooing, chose not to accept the gift of salvation.'

'When I think about the harsh attitude my father had towards God, it seems he will be lost,' Mrs Naumann said, looking depressed.

'*We* don't know that for certain about anyone,' I explained, 'because we cannot look into a person's heart. We don't know, for example, what decision a dying person makes in the last minutes of his or her life and what is said to God in a silent prayer. It doesn't take much time to accept Christ and his salvation. That can even happen in the last hours of a person's life.'

'Do you really think so?'

'I do. We have a biblical example. A criminal on the cross next to Jesus turned to him in the last few hours of his life and asked to be saved for eternity. And Jesus assured him right then and there that he would be in Paradise with him.[4] One thing is certain in any case: God is merciful and just – and he wants to save everyone.'[5]

'But if someone didn't want to know anything about God all his life, wouldn't it be unlikely that he would turn to him in the last minute?'

'If a person has been absolutely indifferent towards God or if he or she has rejected him altogether – in that case you might be right. But such a person wouldn't be happy in a world in which God was at the centre anyway. That person eventually would get what he or she always wanted: to be left alone by God. After all, he was not aiming for eternal life on God's new Earth.'

'Well, that's not much of a comfort,' my neighbour said.

I tried to get my point across from a different angle: 'How did you feel a hundred years ago?'

'That's a funny question. Do I look that old?' She laughed. 'Of course, I didn't feel anything at all. I hadn't even been born.'

'That's how I picture the state of the lost in eternity. They will neither suffer pain, nor will they experience joy. They just will not exist. God will judge each case justly and mercifully.

'That will be demonstrated in this phase of the judgement, and in the end all who are saved will be fully convinced: "God was patient, longsuffering and compassionate. He did the right thing.[6] It was not his fault if a person chose to be lost. The only thing left would have been to force him or her to be saved." But God does not force anyone, because that would contradict his character and wouldn't produce anything positive. He respects our decision. Trust and genuine love can be based only on free choice, as we have stated before.'

'And if a person who is lost never had a chance at all to find God – what about that?' Mrs Naumann added.

'Here, again, we just have to trust in God's goodness. He will make a decision which the saved will review. This is one of the key issues in this judgement: Has God given each particular person a fair chance to be saved? The Bible states clearly: God wants to save every human being. That's why he is searching for each and every one.[7] That's why he knocks on the door of everybody's heart.[8] He has been doing that ever since man's first sin. Even in Paradise he searched for the first two human beings, although they tried to hide from him.'[9]

'As a child I thought it was amusing to imagine how Adam and Eve were hiding from God and how God was pretending he didn't know where they were,' my companion said. 'If God knows everything, why would he have searched for them?'

'I thought that was strange, too, until I realised that by calling them, God tried to bring them to some insight. They were to realise for themselves where their wrong acts had led them. Of course, he knew where they were. But, after all, he does everything possible to appeal to our reason and insight.'

'OK; that way it makes sense.'

'We can see how serious God really is about clearing up all questions and doubts by the fact that he takes a lot of time for the second phase of the judgement. The Bible talks about a period of a thousand years.[10] But that certainly doesn't mean that we'll sit in a courtroom every day for a thousand years. We'll go to those cases which interest us personally or which affect us because they are dealing with our relatives or friends. Some of the saved will be selected for jury duty,[11] while others will be spectators of the proceedings.'

'But won't it be torture to see some of our loved ones sentenced and lost?'

'I'm sure it will be painful and we shall be sad when Christ explains why he couldn't save a loved one. He loved that person even more than we did, though all his efforts were in vain. I'm sure we will cry and mourn for the lost, but God will comfort us and wipe away all our tears. That's what it says in the book of Revelation.'[12]

She looked at me very seriously, contemplatively, but said nothing.

Notes:
[1] Isaiah 65:17-19, 21.
[2] 1 Corinthians 13:12.
[3] John 5:22, 27; 1 Corinthians 6:2, 3; Revelation 20:4a.
[4] Luke 23:39-43; compare to John 20:17.
[5] 1 Timothy 2:4.
[6] Revelation 15:4.
[7] Luke 19:10.
[8] Revelation 3:20.
[9] Genesis 3:8, 9.
[10] Revelation 20:4-7.
[11] Matthew 19:28.
[12] Revelation 21:4.

CHAPTER FOURTEEN

The Rest of the Story

Heavenly Jerusalem and the New Earth

After a few silent moments, I continued.

'Earlier you told me that you had lost your father and your husband.'

'Yes, why?'

'I'm sure, immediately after each loss you were sad, perhaps even desperate, and understandably so. But then after an extended process of mourning which no doubt was painful, you apparently overcame the loss and once again started to enjoy life, right?'

'Exactly. For instance, when I spend some time with my sister in Pittsburgh, as I just have, we have a lot of fun, even though both of us have lost our father. You're right: we can overcome such a loss and then can even think back without any pain. But I have still another question. Does anyone in that court still have a chance that a sentence will be changed from "lost" to "saved"? After all, you said some of the saved would work as jurors. Couldn't they outvote God if things were handled democratically?'

'Fortunately, there will be a theocracy in Heaven, and not a democracy,' I said, slightly amused. 'The rule of the people, and you know that is the meaning of "democracy", has not always brought about the best results. But I don't want to start a political discussion. I want, rather, to answer your question.'

'Please do.'

'OK; I suppose that, in principle, a revision of God's judgement would be possible. Otherwise the whole proceedings would be nothing but a show trial. God is not afraid to submit his decisions to a discussion. When he has presented all of his evidence and given reasons for his decisions, we shall understand that he could not have acted in any other way and that he has not made any mistakes.'

Mrs Naumann looked at me for a long time and then said, 'I hope you are really right and that God does not make any mistakes.' Then, after a pause: 'And what will happen after that? We are still dealing with the second phase of the judgement, aren't we?'

'Yes. I imagine that there will be yet other movie-style presentations in the New Jerusalem. On American radio there is a well-known journalist, Paul Harvey, who likes to tell true anecdotes that, at first, don't appear to be anything special. Only at the end, to the surprise of his listeners, does he connect them with some well-known name or event. And his last sentence is always, "And now you know the rest of the story."

'In this sense God will show us the rest of the story as well. He will show us what was happening behind the scenes of world history; how Satan was at work and to what extent he interfered or restrained himself. He will show us the great controversy between good and evil in many details, and he will explain his actions to us.

'I further imagine that there will be yet other movie-style presentations. They will be in very small rooms with enough space for just two persons – you and your guardian angel, or my guardian angel and me. Our guardian angels will then play our entire lives back to us.'

'I'm sure that would be fascinating,' she said enthusiastically.

'He'll show us the danger we were in at times, without our knowing it, and how he had helped us. We'll also be shown situations in which we were unhappy with God's decisions. Our guardian angel might then say to us, "Do you remember how disappointed you were back then? You thought God had not answered your prayer and you doubted him. But now I'll show you what would have happened had he answered the way you wished." And then we'll have a much better understanding of everything and we'll eventually say with absolute conviction: "God, you are great. Thank you, Lord, that you have led me so wisely and patiently. Now all my questions are answered." '

'That sounds good. But isn't there an easier way?'

'I admit that the entire procedure is complex and time-intensive. But the sin problem with all its consequences cannot be eliminated with just a flick of the finger and thumb. Not even God can do that because he wants to make the universe safe once and for all. There must never be another insurrection. All who have received eternal life must be convinced from the bottom of their hearts that God is compassionate, merciful and just and that they can trust him without reservation. Any doubt about his gracious character could at some point in the future turn us into rebels.'

'Another question just came to my mind. You mentioned the New Jerusalem. What's the story about that? Isn't everything happening in Heaven?'

'It is. But in order to understand this New Jerusalem, we have to turn back for a moment. When Christ returns he will take the saved back to Heaven with him. The earth will be desolate because of the preceding events, especially after an earthquake of a greater magnitude than any we have known up to then.[1] The people who die at the Second Coming will be strewn all over the earth. Nobody will bury them. Satan and his demons will have no interest in that. They will be condemned to inactivity, for they will neither be allowed to leave the earth nor to bother any of God's intelligent beings.[2] They will have 1,000 years to think about what they have accomplished by their rebellion.'

'And the saved?'

'The earth will no longer be a suitable place for habitation. But God has already prepared the New Jerusalem for them in Heaven. In the book of Revelation it is described as a fantastic city, with streets of gold, huge gates made of single pearls and high walls around it made of gems.[3] I'm especially impressed by the size: it's built in a square and one side is approximately 2,220 kilometres or 1,400 miles long.'

'How can you know that so precisely?'

'An angel was given the task of measuring the city. For that he was to use a human measuring unit. In the last but one chapter of the Bible we can read the result: exactly 12,000 stadia.[4] A stadium is the diameter or length of the old Roman arena for chariot races – approximately 185 metres or a little over 203 yards. That's how I arrive at 2,220 kilometres or 1,400 miles. Just imagine that! This city has a length equivalent to the distance from Stockholm to Naples and from London to Moscow, and an area covering all of Europe without Russia.'

'But then there won't be much space for the saved, will there?'

'Oh, yes, there'll be plenty of room. If you take the current population of Berlin, then there will be enough room for more than 20 billion people in this city. And Berlin has many green areas, forests, parks, lakes and only a few high-rise buildings. The holding capacity of the New Jerusalem is considerably bigger. Jesus was not exaggerating when he explained to his disciples that there were "many mansions" in his Father's house.[5] God is apparently making generous plans and wants to save many people. I'm sure he has already reserved a mansion for you as well.'

Mrs Naumann smiled. 'I am afraid that a lot of things will still have to happen in my life, don't you think? At the moment I count myself among the lost.' She paused. 'Doesn't that sound horrible? But on the other hand I, too, would like to rent a place in the New Jerusalem – the way you describe it.'

'That's a good first step in the right direction. Fortunately, we don't have to pay rent. We shall be God's guests, free of charge. I am sure you would be happy there.

'In the New Jerusalem – by the way, named that way because the old Jerusalem with its beautiful temple was God's dwelling place on Earth – I am sure there will be many parks, trees, flowers and lakes. And, especially, there will be avenues of trees with the tree of life growing on both sides of a river with crystal-clear water coming from the throne of God. It will produce fruit every month and we shall be allowed to eat from it.[6]

'Now I should like to explain to you the final act of the trial – the third phase. It will take place after the 1,000 years are over.'

'Please do.'

'First, on Earth, space will be created for the New Jerusalem. It will then come down to Earth together with God and Christ.[7]

'After that the second resurrection will take place in which all the lost will come back to life. God will then present the plan of salvation in some detail before them. In particular, he will show what Christ did on Earth and what he suffered at the Cross. All human beings will see exactly what God has done for their salvation. Yet their hearts will be so hardened that even this extraordinary presentation of the plan of salvation will not move them to turn to God. But they will feel compelled to acknowledge the power and goodness of God and thus confirm the correctness of his decisions.[8] Even Satan will do that. But he will not do it out of love for God but because he feels compelled to do so.'

'Interesting.'

'Thus it will be demonstrated for all intelligent creatures, the onlooking universe, the saved and the lost, including Satan, that God's actions were just and loving and that the lost and all demons have neither the right nor the qualification for eternal life. God will be fully vindicated before all intelligent beings. Thus the final act can happen.'

'The destruction we mentioned earlier.'

'Basically, yes. In Revelation we have a description of how Satan is not going to give up without a fight. He claims that he has resurrected the lost and persuades them to believe that they can take the New Jerusalem by force.[9] After all, they are greater in number. And some of the best military leaders of all time will be by his side.

'Thus, one more time, Satan's true character as a seducer, liar and murderer becomes evident. For the second time he will plan the murder of God. But in the middle of the preparations the throne of God will be lifted up above the New Jerusalem and the Father and the Son will show themselves in their entire glory. That, the lost cannot endure. They will perish, just as the demons and Satan, too. That way evil will be eradicated at its roots.'

'I am sure God will be glad about that.'

'Yes and no. He loves all his creatures, even though they have turned away from him. Therefore, even God will shed tears over all the lost angels and people.

'Apart from the crucifixion of Jesus, this will be the saddest episode in the history of the universe. But in the book of Revelation it says that God will wipe away all our tears.[10] We shall all mourn together over the great loss, but eventually – as with any process of mourning – we shall overcome the loss and find new joy in living.'

'I think I should cry a lot, if I were to be there.'

'Yes, I'm sure that I'll cry about some family members and friends. But eventually the pain will be gone for good. God has promised that.'

'And with that everything is done?'

'After that, only one thing remains for God to do. With an incredible fire, the entire earth will be cleansed from all traces of sin and, finally, in a creative act, it will be renewed.[11] It will become a Paradise. Then each one of the saved will be able to live in his or her own home. But considering the pleasant climate on the new earth we shall not depend on that. We shall be able to dwell anywhere out in the open.

'But I'm not sure whether we'll need any sleep at all. In any case, there will never be any darkness on the new earth. We shan't need the sun anymore, because God will be our light. That's the way it's described in the book of Revelation.'[12]

'And what shall we do all day long?'

'There will be many possibilities of which we have as yet no idea. Some of the things we mentioned earlier. I picture it in very concrete terms: I should like to play with lions and other animals who are ferocious and dangerous here on Earth. There, the Bible says, they will be peaceful and eat grass.'[13]

'What else?'

'I'm sure we'll be able to travel around the universe, too. Perhaps we shall be able to beam ourselves from one place to another, as depicted in some science-fiction movies. I am especially interested in visiting other worlds. What kinds of beings has God created there? How has their history unfolded?

'And I'm sure these beings will be interested in us and our experiences here. They can at last talk to those about whom they have heard so many things for so long and whom they have watched on the inter-galactic television network. I'm talking about God's news channel, featuring the progress of the controversy here on Earth.'

'Isn't your imagination getting the better of you now?' laughed Mrs Naumann.

'I don't think so. Paul writes that we humans have become a spectacle for other worlds.[14] Therefore, we can conclude that their inhabitants who have remained loyal to God are able to observe this controversy. In what detail, of course, I don't know. I hope, however, that they haven't been watching me too closely, if you know what I mean! But in any case it's always more interesting to talk to an actor personally than just to watch him on the screen. That's why talk shows with famous people are so popular today. Perhaps we'll be doing something similar. I don't know.'

'You have it all worked out, haven't you?'

'Well, I believe I have biblical reasons for believing these things. And there's still more.'

'Please.'

'We'll not only see and hear Christ but we'll be able to talk with him in person. That will be a very special experience, when I shall have a personal "audience" with Christ. I am afraid I shall not be able to say too much. I'll probably just stammer, "Thank you. Thank you. Thank you." But, after all, Jesus knows my thoughts and my love for him now anyway.'

My neighbour looked at me, searching my face. I could not tell from her expression what she was thinking. I should have loved to know, but I didn't ask.

Notes:
[1] Revelation 16:17, 18.
[2] Revelation 20:1-3.
[3] Revelation 21:10-21.
[4] Revelation 21:16.
[5] John 14:2, 3.
[6] Revelation 22:1, 2.
[7] Revelation 21:2.
[8] Revelation 15:4.
[9] Revelation 20:7-9.
[10] Revelation 21:4.
[11] 2 Peter 3:10-13.
[12] Revelation 21:23; 22:5.
[13] Isaiah 65:25.
[14] 1 Corinthians 4:9.

CHAPTER FIFTEEN

How Would You Like to Die?

The conversion experience and its consequences

At that time the captain made an announcement. He asked us to put on our seatbelts. About thirty seconds later we hit some heavy turbulence. Each time the aircraft plummeted, groans went through the cabin. The flight attendants went to their seats and buckled up.

I noticed that Mrs Naumann became a little pale, and not until we had reached more stable air masses did colour return to her face.

'Turbulence frightens me to death,' she said, 'even though I know that take-offs and landings are much more dangerous.'

I looked at her: 'If you had a choice, what would be your preferred way of dying?'

She thought about it for a while. 'If I had a choice, I really should like to die in old age, in good health, in my sleep. Then I shouldn't feel anything.'

'Most people to whom I have put the same question want that, too. As far as old age and good health are concerned, I agree. But I should like to have the opportunity before I die to put things right with God and my fellow men, if I need to.'

'Why is that so important to you?'

'Well, let me tell you a story that I heard which will explain it. Through some personal contacts a friend learned about the results from a black box voice recorder after a plane crash.

'Seven to eight minutes before the impact the crew and the passengers knew that they would die in a short time. But then a pastor's wife went to the microphone and basically made the following announcement: "My friends, in a few minutes our lives will come to an end. Our fate is virtually sealed. But this need not be the absolute end for us. If you like, in the remaining minutes I shall share with you how each one of us can receive eternal life.

"Through our sins we have separated ourselves from God. Because of that we shall all die – we have inherited eternal death. God, our Creator, however, loves us so much that he sent his own Son, Jesus Christ, to Earth. He lived a life without sin and even though he did not deserve to die, he died for all of us. He became our substitute and suffered the punishment for our mistakes. Through his act on our behalf, our guilt can be forgiven. All we have to do is trust in Jesus as our Saviour and Lord and confess to him all our sins, our wrong attitudes and our wrong behaviour. It doesn't matter how much or how little we have sinned or how big our sins were. They will all be forgiven and, through Christ's merits, we shall then stand before God as if we had never sinned, and eternal life will be given to us at the Second Coming of Christ without our deserving it. God will give a new body to each one of us and we, as his children, shall live on the new earth forever. That's what he has promised." '

'Amazing,' Mrs Naumann said, transfixed.

'Then the lady invited all the passengers, who were willing, to pray with her. Shortly after that, the recording was interrupted.'

Mrs Naumann was visibly touched.

'I don't know how many accepted that last-minute offer,' I continued, 'but I think there must have been some.

'How exciting it will be when we – and I hope both of us shall be there – shall stroll through the parks of the heavenly Jerusalem and meet someone who will tell us that without that dramatic experience he or she would never have received eternal life. That person will certainly be grateful to the pastor's wife – literally forever.'

'I can see that for some it can be a blessing to know beforehand that they will die a little later,' she said, deep in thought.

'It would certainly be better to put things right with God long before that time, because very few of us know in advance when we shall die.'

'That's true. A little over six months ago my cousin died. We were very close. One moment she was alive and happy and then, all of a sudden, she was dead. She was not very old – two years younger than I. She died of a heart attack in the evening. In the afternoon of the same day we had been on a walk and had some coffee and cake. I could hardly comprehend it.'

'Unfortunately, there is no guarantee of a long life here. But in the

Bible it says that in our lives God will somehow give every person opportunities to make decisions for him.[1] A procedure, as we discussed earlier, he will reveal to us one day in court. God is fair and merciful. He is trying to do whatever he can so that each human being will be saved. Nobody needs to be lost.'

'How do I know that God wants to reach me?'

I was happy about that question. 'Don't you feel it this very moment? If we seriously think about our relationship with God, or if our conscience is bothering us and telling us that we should put things right with God and our fellowman, then that is a sure sign that the Spirit of God is working on us. God never misses a chance to reach us. He uses different ways: a conversation like this one, a book or a painful experience. I am convinced that God has sufficient opportunities to make us aware that our relationship with him is not in order and that we should turn to him.'

'But if I should decide for Christ today, I should always feel that something was missing – a lot of fun in life,' Mrs Naumann said. 'In that case, I couldn't enjoy so many things. For that reason alone I should rather wait.'

I had to smile. 'I know what you mean. In the past, before I decided to live a life with Christ, I thought the same way. But today I see things quite differently, because I have learned that the opposite is true. After my decision to commit my life to Christ, the quality of my life improved dramatically. That's why I am so grateful to God that I got to know him in my youth.'

'In what way has your life improved?'

'Since my conversion I have peace with God. Jesus has become my best friend. He has freed me from wrong habits and harmful dependencies, and he has removed in me any fear of the future. He gives me assurance so that I can start every day with optimism. I know that he is by my side, for he has promised, "I will be with you always to the end of the world."[2] I rely on that promise. I can talk to him in prayer and ask him for help. And he has never let me down.'

She looked at me in disbelief. 'Are you trying to say that you haven't had any problems since, that you're living only on the sunny side of life?'

'No, that's not what I mean, not at all. There will always be problems. On the one hand, I'm not perfect. I still make mistakes. On the other hand, after his or her conversion, every genuine Christian becomes a target for Satan. After all, we are involved in a great controversy between him and God.

'What should give us comfort, however, is the fact that when we are on Christ's side of the battle, we belong to the victorious team. Jesus is by our side and fights for us. He helps us to master any and all of life's crises. And, as you believe yourself, he has placed a guardian angel at our side.

'Besides that, I belong to a worldwide Church. This means a lot to me. I count many Christians among my friends. I can trust them and they are there for me when I need help. They also pray for me.'

'But doesn't conversion also mean that I shall no longer be allowed to do certain things?'

'In a way, yes. But that's not the point. Because now many things I do not *want* to do anymore, because my values have changed. Many things which were once important to me are today no longer important – and vice-versa.'

'For example?'

'I used to party a lot. I danced till late at night or into the morning and I also used to drink alcohol. It is different today. Even though I still enjoy happy get-togethers, my taste in music has changed and I prefer to spend my nights in bed. And I no longer need alcohol to be happy.

'Today I live differently and I am better off than before. My life now has a stable foundation and clear goals and focus. And I feel a deep peace. That alone is worth a lot.'

My neighbour thought for a while and then cautiously said, 'I should like to ask you something. But I don't want to intrude.'

'Just go ahead and ask.'

'You just mentioned that Christ has freed you from bad habits and dependencies. You don't have to tell me this – perhaps it's too personal. But could you at least give me a hint as to what you meant by that?'

'Sure. During puberty – I must have been around 12 or 13 years old – I got into the habit of stealing, shoplifting. In my case it had developed into a real sport. I am not talking about big things. In most cases they were toys, like little model cars, or sweets. I had become quite adept at it, too. Nobody ever caught me.

'But one day, to my horror, I noticed that I no longer had any choice in the matter. I felt compelled to reach for things, even if I didn't want to. Stealing had become second nature to me. It was compulsive. I don't know whether this was a case of kleptomania, but in any case I wasn't far from it. I was quite concerned. I became aware of the fact that I was dependent – dependent on a bad habit.'

'And how did you become free?'

'My mother had told me about God and Jesus Christ. From her I knew how to pray and what prayer could accomplish.'

'So you come from a Christian home?'

'Yes, my parents were Christians. Looking back today, I wish they had told me even more about God. My mother had a closer relationship with God than my father. But she communicated her Christian values through deeds rather than words. But through her I had some basic Christian understanding.

'In any case, back then I didn't know of any other way out than to go to my room, get on my knees and pray to God. I said, "Dear God, if you are for real and if you are almighty and you care about me, then please forgive me my sins and free me from this compulsion to steal. And if you answer my prayer, I want to belong to you from now on. Amen."

'I was really serious. After that I was wondering what would happen. Would God answer my prayer? Does prayer work at all? Does God care about me?'

'It worked?'

'Yes, it was great. From that moment on, after that prayer, my dependency was gone. I didn't have to steal anymore, and I've never done it since. That was history – once and for all. God actually and literally freed me.

'That was the beginning of my life with Christ. After that I read the Bible frequently and I became better and better acquainted with Jesus. When I was almost 17, I made my decision public and, at my own request, was baptised.'

'You hadn't already been baptised?' Mrs Naumann asked in surprise.

'No. My parents were of the opinion that baptism required a conscious decision on the part of the one being baptised and that one first had to believe before taking that step. My mother quite often quoted Jesus by saying, "Whoever believes and is baptised will be saved."[3] And because babies can neither believe in God nor make a decision for him, my parents didn't want to have me baptised as a baby. For that, later on, I was grateful to them because, as I understand the Bible today, they were right. Perhaps their decision to some extent was also motivated by the fact that they belonged to different churches. In not having us children baptised as babies they avoided a conflict.'

Notes:
[1] Job 33:29, 30.
[2] Matthew 28:20.
[3] Mark 16:16.

CHAPTER SIXTEEN

Freedom in the No-smoking Section

Conversion, repentance and rebirth

'Earlier on you were talking about conversion,' Mrs Naumann said. 'Could you explain it more fully?'

'Sure,' I said, glad to get on to what I believe is a crucial topic. 'This is an important subject because it deals with the question of how we personally experience salvation through Jesus Christ. Conversion refers to a turning around to God. I had been running away from him, I had turned my back on him, or I just hadn't cared about him. Based on certain experiences or insights, I had then been awakened inside and decided to give up my rebellion or indifference, build a relationship with God, and live in harmony with him. This basic change of direction is what the Bible calls "conversion".'

'And what does that have to do with repentance?'

'The biblical understanding of repentance is at the heart of conversion. The word "repentance" in the New Testament means "change of mind", a changed way of thinking about God, which results in a turning around to him.'

'And that has nothing to do with our actions?'

'I sometimes say, "Doing repentance has nothing to do with any kind of doing at all." '

'What's that again?'

'Just playing a little. Seriously, though, repentance is more about our attitude, our sorrow about our former relationship with God. When I realised that I had been heading in the wrong direction, made many mistakes, and rejected God's love or just completely ignored him, I then became remorseful over that and had a change of heart. Or when I experienced God in a special way and became aware of his love, that would awaken emotions which could lead me to a change of direction. I then became more open to the working of the Holy Spirit. I now have genuine remorse about my past actions and attitudes. These are the best motives for a thorough conversion. At the heart of it there will always be a decision of the mind and the heart.'

'I still don't fully understand that.' My neighbour again looked at me with a wrinkled forehead.

'Even someone who has experienced it does not quite fully understand it. We can neither comprehend nor explain the working of the Holy Spirit. We can only experience and describe it. When we accept Christ as our Saviour and Lord, God's Spirit will cause some kind of a spiritual rebirth or new birth in us.[1] Jesus himself once used this illustration.'[2]

'Yes, I've heard of being born again.'

'There are different views. In the eastern religions they have a completely different concept from what Jesus meant. He was talking about an inner event, an inner re-creation, through which we become children of God. We receive the ability to establish a close relationship with God. After that we can understand him better, trust him and love him. We suddenly have the inner desire to please him and to listen to him.'

'I see. We listen and obey, I take it?'

'Exactly. Our earthly parents expect their children to listen to and obey them – at least when they're young. With God it works somewhat differently.'

'It does? How is that?'

'Through his Spirit, in the new birth he plants in our hearts his principles and commandments. This is God's doing. They then are no longer a burden. We even experience joy when we obey.'

'That's hard to imagine!'

'I understand. Only someone who has experienced it himself or herself knows what I am talking about here. Otherwise, it does sound strange.'

'Really.'

'Let me give you an example of what I mean.'

'Please do, by all means.'

'You probably don't smoke, right?'

'Right. And during the flight we are not allowed to smoke anyway.'

'Do you feel that this is a restriction of your freedom?'

'Not at all. On the contrary.'

'And when you board a train, in which section will you look for a seat?'

'In the no-smoking section, of course. The air is much better there. What are you getting at?'

'Even though smoking is prohibited in that section, you, more or less consciously, say to yourself, "This is where I want to be. This is where I shall feel comfortable." You don't think, "I can't stand it! Always these forbidden things! I feel so restricted!" '

'In that particular case, of course not.'

'Yet for a smoker the situation is quite different, right? The smoker will feel uncomfortable in the no-smoking section, restricted in freedom. If the smoker gives up smoking, converts from a smoker to a non-smoker, that person will then feel as comfortable among non-smokers as you or I do, right?'

I paused. Since my companion only looked at me, I continued. 'It's like that when it comes to God's commandments. Once we are converted and are born again, we are happy to keep them.[3] We shall even *want* to keep them.'

'So the keeping of the commandments is important to be saved, is it not? Did I understand you correctly that way?'

'Well, you have to be careful here not to confuse cause and effect. By keeping the commandments we cannot collect brownie points with God, or even earn eternal life. It's way too late for our obedience to the law to save any of us. We shall be saved only through Christ's merits, which we claim for ourselves.'[4]

She looked at me in a puzzled way.

'When we have been converted and are born anew, we have been saved from sin, from being lost, from meaninglessness and hopelessness. Then, afterwards, the *effect* will give us new motives, and a new source of strength. We'll then conform to the will of God. That is the *result* of my salvation. But the keeping of the commandments is not the precondition for my being saved. Rather, it's what I do after I have been saved.'

'That sounds logical, though I have to say it's also a bit complicated, at least for a person like me,' Mrs Naumann said. 'I hope that I won't have forgotten all this by tomorrow.'

'Perhaps a comparison will help. If I really love a person, I shall not find it difficult to do whatever it takes to maintain harmony between us. I shall strive to read from her eyes her every wish, and be grateful if she explains to me what is important to her and how I can make her happy.'

'Sounds like a great relationship.'

'Precisely. And that's what it's supposed to be. It is quite similar in our relationship with God. Once we realise how much he loves us and that he has our best interests at heart, we start to love God, a love driven by a changed heart, a love expressed in a real and tangible way. Jesus expresses it by saying, "If you love me keep my commandments."[5] The correct translation actually says, "If you love me you will keep my commandments." '

'So we obey, not to try to earn salvation but because, well, we already have it, and because we have salvation, we love God?'

'Yes, and we reveal that love by keeping his commandments. It really is that simple.'

Notes:
[1] John 1:12, 13.
[2] John 3:3-8.
[3] Psalms 40:8.
[4] Romans 3:23, 24, 28.
[5] John 14:15.

CHAPTER SEVENTEEN

Why is God Nice to Evil People?

God's mercy and blessings

My co-passenger reached for a plastic cup from the flight attendant's tray.

She took a long swig before finally setting the empty cup down.

'I don't know what to say,' she replied, looking at me. 'All of this is so new. Nobody has ever explained it to me like this before.'

'Does it make sense?'

'Most of it, yes. More than I could have ever imagined.'

'What, though, do you still find troubling?'

'In the beginning I said that I don't understand why God treats some bad people so well.'

'Fair enough question. Let's look at it.'

'Please, do.'

'Of course, for starters, it bothers our sense of justice when good people suffer and evil people appear to do well. In some cases, their material prosperity, their success, was not acquired legally. Some bad guy might do really well but at the expense of innocent people.'

'Right, and so I want to know: How can God let that happen if he is just?'

'Well, Mrs Naumann, early on we found out that, in a sense, God *has* to let it happen in order for it to become clear to everyone where evil leads. If he interfered in all those cases, Satan could call that unfair. Besides, if God always intervened, the true character of sin would never be revealed. It is sin, after all, which causes everyone's suffering, even that of the so-called innocent.'

'What do you mean by so-called?'

'Well, in some cases, those who are lied to, cheated or stolen from might have brought it upon themselves. Perhaps they have treated others the same way. But I have to admit that in most cases the victims are innocent.'

'For sure.'

'In the case of believers who lead respectable lives and yet suffer, other factors are at work. Whoever converts to Christ, and, by doing so, changes sides in the great controversy, will become a target for Satan, who now tries to make life difficult for the Christian. He does that to try to discourage people and thus turn them away.

'An especially harsh example of this is found in the Bible – the story of Job. He's someone who even God said was respectable and who avoided all evil. That caused Satan to claim that Job served God only because he had blessed him so richly; that is, Job served God only from selfish motives. If everything were to be taken from him, Satan argued, Job would renounce God and become unfaithful to him.'[1]

'Yes, I have heard of the story, but don't know it well.'

'OK, but in this situation, with Satan making those accusations, who alone could prove who was right?'

'What do you mean?'

'God claimed that Job loved him, and Satan claimed that Job served God for selfish reasons. Who alone could provide the answer of who was right, God or Satan?'

'Only Job himself could say what his motives were.'

'Yes. But Satan would not have been satisfied with a mere claim by Job. Evidence had to be given.'

'So Job had to be put to the test?'

'Exactly. If God wanted to remain fair towards Satan, there was *no other option* than to allow Satan to put Job to the test.[2] For the sake of justice, God *could not* stop Job from suffering.'

'That's a strange kind of justice!'

'So it seems. But we know that kind of dilemma from earthly court trials. What is justice for the defendant is not always just towards the victim. We cannot create perfect justice, and in the face of Satan's rule on Earth[3] God cannot do this either, at least not now.'

'That's very unsatisfactory.'

'It is for God, too. That's why he's working towards the permanent solution that we talked about earlier. One day we'll see full and final justice.'

'What happened to Job?'

'He lost his possessions, his children and also his health – everything. He received one terrible blow after the other.[4] But, in the end, he did not renounce God. Instead, even in his suffering, Job clung to him and, by so doing, proved Satan wrong.'

'But I don't quite get it.'

'Ultimately, it was about Satan's claim that God was a dictator whom people did not love but served out of fear or for their own advantage.'

'Now I understand: Satan accused Job of worshipping God only because he was benefiting from it.'

'Yes, precisely! And after it was demonstrated, beyond a shadow of a doubt I might add, that Satan was wrong with his slander, God was able once again to bless Job in a visible way. He again gave him children and twice as many possessions as before.'[5]

'I see.'

'Job is a good example to all genuine Christians. They, too, in times of difficulties and suffering have to demonstrate what really motivates them to serve God. That's why God allows some attacks from Satan.'

Mrs Naumann looked at me rather sceptically, but said nothing, so I continued.

'Let's now deal with the other side, the fact that some people prosper, even though they have no relationship with God. God tries to reach them through all kinds of different ways and means, and that's because he wants to save them. He wants to show them how much he loves them. As we know, love is a better motivation for coming to God than fear or desperation.'

'Of course.'

'Paul points out an important principle. He says that God's goodness leads us to *a change of heart*.[6] His blessing, which unbelievers experience as well as believers, is no evidence for the assumption that everything is fine with them. God loves all his creatures. That's why he wants to give them good things. Therefore, he tries to convince them of his love and goodness. He wants them to open up to him.'

'Are you saying that God blesses the unbeliever more than the believer?'

'No. The sun shines and the rain falls on the good and the bad equally.[7] God is just; he doesn't favour anyone. But with genuine followers of Jesus the blessing may not be as obvious. Most of all they will receive a spiritual blessing.[8] This includes the forgiveness of guilt, inner peace, strength in temptations, wisdom in critical decisions and so forth.[9] A non-Christian is not receptive to these kinds of blessings.

'Besides that, in the question of God's blessings, Satan's lies also play an important role. He claims that God treats the unbeliever unkindly. But that is exactly what he doesn't do. On the contrary: he is love personified,[10] and as such he shows all his creatures – wherever possible – his great love. But in the process of doing so he *cannot* and *must not* nullify the law of cause and effect. He will not annul the consequences of man's actions and Satan's workings. But one day he will put an end to all evil, and will do so in a way that will convince everyone, even the devil himself, that God dealt with sin and rebellion in a fair, just and loving manner.'

My co-passenger said nothing but was deep in thought.

Notes:
[1] Job 1:1-3, 6-11.
[2] Job 1:12; 2:6, 7.
[3] 2 Corinthians 4:4.
[4] Job 1:13-22; 2:4-10.
[5] Job 42:12-17.
[6] Romans 2:4.
[7] Matthew 5:45.
[8] Ephesians 1:3.
[9] Ephesians 1:7, 11; 1 John 1:9; 5:11-13; Romans 5:1, 2.
[10] 1 John 4:8, 16.

CHAPTER EIGHTEEN

A Dangerous Mountain Hike

Saving faith

'When you were talking about eternal life before, I really felt a longing for Heaven,' she said. 'For you the whole thing seems to be so certain. I envy you, I mean, that you can believe so firmly. I just can't. Perhaps I am lacking the gift of faith. After all, not everyone has faith.'

'You're right. Even the Bible says that, almost verbatim.'[1]

'Really?'

'Yes, but it has a different meaning from what you think.'

'I'm curious.'

'Paul says, "Faith comes from hearing". The word translated "faith" in Greek, the language of the New Testament, does not mean only "trust" but also "faithfulness". The context of this verse shows that faithfulness is referred to. In some translations it reads, "for not all are faithful".[2] Whether or not we are faithful depends, really, on us, on the choices we make. Because God is a good life partner, we really have no good reason to leave him.'

'But how can I find God if I feel so far from him?'

'You need a personal relationship with him. That's the key. Faith comes by hearing, says Paul, and hearing the Christian message comes by the Word of God.[3] And Peter says that the seed which brings forth the new birth is the Word of God.[4] In other words, we must, by all means, deal with the source, the Word of God, so that faith can develop and grow.'

'I see.'

'In the biblical sense, faith means to trust God and Jesus Christ, and for that the Bible is indispensable because it shows us what God is really like. Ideally, we should start reading the gospels. There we can see the clearest representation of God in Jesus Christ. We can simply

put ourselves in the shoes of the folks there. For what Jesus said to the people back then he would say to us in a similar situation. And the way he treated people back then is the way he would treat us now.'

'That makes sense.'

'We learn to trust God in much the same way we learn to trust people. I'm sure you have friends.'

'Sure. But, unfortunately, I don't see them often enough.'

'Do you also have a best friend?'

'Oh, yes. She lives in Düsseldorf.'

'How long have you known her?'

'We have been friends forever, it seems. Or at least forty years. But we've been really close for about twenty-six of those forty.'

'How did that closeness come about, if you don't mind my asking?'

'No, not at all. My husband was very sick back then. Had cancer and was in great pain. I had to be by his side the whole time. During those days my friend, who lived just two blocks away, helped me tremendously. She took care of our household and my son. We often had long conversations. Back then I really needed that emotional support. It was a difficult time, as you can imagine, and she was there for me.'

'Good. And that's when you learned that you could trust her and that's when you became close?'

'Yes.'

'It's really very similar with God. Perhaps for a long time he may be like somebody we have heard about. But then, all of a sudden, we get to know him personally – triggered perhaps by a crisis, or because of the influence of a Christian. We then start dealing with him more closely, perhaps through a conversation like this one we've been having.'

'Interesting . . . '

'You see, whoever gets to know God and finds out what he is really like knows that he/she can trust him, no matter what. And the better we get to know him, and the more time we spend with him – as you did with your friend – the more we trust. This is the secret of saving faith.'

'And this faith will save me?'

'Yes and no,' I said. 'I should like to explain this with the help of a drawing.' I got up, opened the overhead compartment and took a notepad out of my briefcase. After sitting down again, I drew the picture of a train with an attached passenger carriage followed by a coal wagon. Then I connected the carriage to the engine with a plus sign.

While I was writing the word 'Christ' on the engine and the word 'I' on the carriage, I explained, 'Christ is the engine and I am the carriage. The plus sign, however, this hitch, that is my faith.' I drew a circle around the plus sign and wrote the word 'faith' below it.

'It is not my faith which saves me, but Jesus Christ. It is not the hitch which is pulling me, but the engine. My faith is merely the means that connects me to Christ. Based on my trust, I hold on to Christ and remain faithful to him. Then, through Christ, I shall be saved for eternity.'

'And what about the coal wagon? Is that where my sins go?'

I laughed. 'That completes this illustration. When you choose Christ and connect with him through faith, then, in a way, you do throw all your guilt into the coal truck. Then you are rid of it. And if you commit another sin, you do it again. Christ, so to speak, turns the black dirt of my sin into the white steam of his cleanness. He knows that we shall continue to make mistakes and need time to mature as children of God and that we'll learn from our mistakes and acquire new patterns of behaviour.'

'That's encouraging.'

'In this context, I should like to point out something about the role of feelings, too, because that's important.'

'Please, go ahead.'

'Often our feelings can be quite pleasant, especially during our early days as believers in Jesus. But they also can be influenced quite easily by circumstances, negative experiences, or stress. We must know, however, that they play a secondary role. The facts of salvation are first and foremost: Christ paid the penalty for my guilt a long time ago and therefore he can forgive me any sin. These facts are true, no matter what my feelings or even my mind is telling me.'

'Faith is not feeling then? Is that what you're saying?'

'Yes, faith involves feelings, but it transcends them. That is, if I trust in Christ and his salvation, I shall continue to abide in him, even if at times I feel bad. Figuratively speaking, I stay connected to the engine, no matter how I feel.'

'I see.'

'Good feelings come and go, as we all know. That's why we must trust in the facts of salvation more than we do our feelings.'

'Why are you stressing that so much?'

'Because there are many Christians who are not sure about their faith. They doubt that their conversion is genuine. They think some type of religious feeling is the precondition for their faith or their salvation. And if they don't have the expected feeling, then they think God has not accepted them or doesn't love them.'

'I think I understand.'

'Look at it this way, too. Imagine that you are on a hike up in the mountains and you are walking on a narrow crest along a very deep chasm. A fall would certainly be deadly. But you are not alone. In your group are some people whom you don't know personally. All of a sudden somebody among them trips you. You stumble and fall over the cliff – and barely manage to hold on. But your strength is fading quickly. You are facing certain death.'

'That's nice.'

'In this situation you hear a friendly voice above you: "Give me your hand. I will pull you up." What will you do in this situation? Will you say, "No, thanks. I'll manage on my own," or "I don't trust you," or "I don't believe you can do that"?'

'Of course, I shall quickly reach for the hand.'

'Certainly. Then you continue with your climb. This time, as a precaution, you will hold on to the hand of the one who has saved you. That, however, will not keep the one who tripped you from doing it again. This time you stumble but you don't fall.

'Perhaps after a while you become overly confident and you let go of your new friend's hand. Again your adversary trips you and you again fall. But, fortunately, your friend again offers you his hand. You immediately grab it and allow him to save you. You trust him because you have experienced his trustworthiness.'

'And what are you trying to illustrate by that?'

'As human beings we are in a similar situation. Satan has tripped all of us. He has incited us into rebelling against God, or he has caused us to neglect God and do our own things, no matter how contrary to God's will. We are all hanging above a chasm. We do not have to make a conscious choice for Satan in order to be lost for eternity. By not choosing sides we have already chosen sides. We are already subject to death. If we do not choose the saving hand of Jesus, we fall into the chasm.'

'Very heavy, I must say.'

'Yes, it is. Jesus Christ is offering us his hand because he wants to save us. We have only to decide to grab his hand and to hold on to it.'

'But how does that happen in a concrete way?'

'The grabbing of Christ's hand illustrates the nature of faith. We have to reach out and trust him and his promises. Somebody had come to Christ but had a problem trusting that Christ would be able to heal his child. Jesus pointed out to him the importance of trusting in him. That's when the father said, "I believe; help my unbelief!"[5] With the little trust he had he clung to Jesus and hoped that he would strengthen his faith. Of course, Jesus did just that – by healing the child, I might add. In other words, Jesus will strengthen our faith as well and grant us positive experiences with him if we accept his offer of salvation and cling to his outstretched hand.'

'But how about Job? What kind of "positive experience" was that, after all?'

'For Job it was, actually.'

She looked at me in surprise.

'At least that's the way Job himself saw it at the very end. Here, read for yourself what he said to God.'

I opened the Bible and looked up Job chapter 42 and pointed to verse 5. Quoting Job's words, I read to her: ' "I have heard of you by the hearing of the ear, but now my eye sees you." However horrible his experience, Job learned some valuable lessons and through that experience had become acquainted with God much more closely.'

She didn't respond.

'Look, I don't want to give you the wrong idea here. A life with God is not just a walk on the sunny side all the time. We've already talked about the reasons for that. But in any case, for a person who has made a decision for Christ, the very experiences in suffering and adversities will strengthen his or her faith.'

'I see.'

'When we have had such experiences with God, our attitudes and our lives will be changed. That's what happened to Job. In his suffering he had accused God and demanded justice for himself. But then he confessed that he had "uttered what I did not understand" and said, "Therefore I abhor myself, and repent in dust and ashes."[6] He became very humble before God. So it's not just our pleasant experiences that help us to continue our walk with Christ. Even the bad ones can as well.'

'There are so many things I still don't understand,' she said, shaking her head.

'I've been walking with God for decades and there's still a lot I don't understand. But even if we do not fully understand Christ, we should trust him and obey his commandments. This trust will be rewarded and thus strengthened. And even through terrible trials our relationship with him can grow.'

'So far I have had a different concept of the word "faith",' she said, 'but now it has become much clearer. I always thought you needed a certain talent for believing, or some special training at least.'

'Well, some people really do have great difficulties in trusting God,' I conceded. 'In their case, during childhood, through parental neglect or even worse, their ability to trust may have developed insufficiently. Or it was destroyed through some bad experiences. For example, emotional or sexual abuse in children will destroy their ability to trust others.

'I only recently became aware of the fact that also through the experience of rejection, that is, through divorce or mistakes in their upbringing, many find it hard to develop a trusting relationship with God. In that case, too, it would be necessary first to deal with the past. Only then could they learn to trust other people – and God.'

'Fortunately,' Mrs Naumann said, 'I had a pretty harmonious and happy relationship with my parents – even though sometimes they put a little too much pressure on me.'

'In that case you should not find it too hard to develop a similar or even better relationship with God and Jesus Christ. When we deal with God and get to know him better, our trust in him will grow automatically. We shall be disappointed only if we have wrong ideas about God and how he works in our lives. That's important because many people, I believe, who reject God do so only because they have wrong ideas about him.'

After that, I kept quiet for a while.

Notes:
[1] 2 Thessalonians 3:2.
[2] Same text in another translation.
[3] Romans 10:17.
[4] 1 Peter 1:23.
[5] Mark 9:22-24, NKJV.
[6] Job 42:3, 5, 6, NKJV.

CHAPTER NINETEEN

Life Motto of a Die-hard

God's love

Not long after the silence began, she broke it.

'How come you know so much about God? Did you get all that from the Bible?'

'Basically, yes. And from some good books, too. Unfortunately, the Bible is not ordered as systematically as I have presented and explained everything to you. The books of the Old Testament mainly contain reports about the history of Israel or the messages by the prophets to a disobedient people.

'Even in the New Testament we find only a few systematic treatises about basic issues relating to faith. The gospels all deal with the life of Jesus, and the letters by the apostles, mostly with church matters. From these we can learn a lot, but the Bible is not a systematic textbook.'

'What do you mean?'

'Well, statements about specific subjects are scattered about. We have to put them together, like a puzzle.'

'So one needs help in any case to find one's way through the Bible, doesn't one?'

'Yes, you can say that. If I hadn't had help, I wouldn't have been in a position to explain those things to you today. And some of them I have learned to understand better myself only recently through a good friend. This has a history, too. The first Christians didn't distribute hand-written copies of the Scriptures but instead they explained to others what faith in Christ was all about. Jesus did the same thing when teaching his disciples. He explained to them the context and in the process referred to the texts in the Old Testament.'[1]

'I guess I should start reading the Bible myself.'

'I'm sure now you will be able to understand things much better than before. I suggest that you start with the gospels – Matthew, Mark or Luke. That's where you get to know Jesus Christ. Concentrate initially on nothing else. That's where you'll find many things that will encourage you to trust him.'

'The gospels, you say?'

'Yes. And my favourite story in the Bible, by the way, is in the gospels, a parable that Jesus told. You probably know it: the one about the prodigal or lost son.'

I looked at my neighbour.

'Sure, I've heard of it but you'd better refresh my memory.'

'A young man demanded from his rich father his inheritance – and actually received it,' I told her. 'He wanted to move abroad. There he wasted his entire fortune together with false friends. Eventually he ended up in bitter poverty. In addition there was a severe famine in that country, and he ended up herding pigs,[2] and for a Jew that was the lowest humiliation possible. Out of pure desperation and need he even was willing to eat pig food.'

'Yuk!'

'For sure. At some point it struck him that even his father's hired help were better off than he was. He made up his mind to return and confess to his father that he had acted wrongly. He wanted to ask his father to employ him as a day-labourer. On his way home he pondered and rehearsed over and over again what he wanted to say.[3] He had, however, completely misjudged his father. He didn't have to stand in front of his father's door as a penitent, begging for forgiveness. The father had waited for his son's return every day, and he had already seen him from afar. But he did not just stand there; he ran towards him.[4] For a Jew back then, that was considered undignified. Jewish men walked with a measured step.

'And before the son could even open his mouth to present his well-rehearsed confession, his father embraced him and kissed him. He barely gave him a chance to say anything. Instead he had the best robe brought out and a signet ring which he put on his finger. He reinstated him as his son and shouted, "This my son was dead and is alive again; he was lost and is found." And they began to be merry.'[5]

'Yes, I know that story. It's beautiful – and really touching.'

'And God is just like that father. Even if we have turned our backs on him intentionally, have misused his talents and have lived an immoral life – if we return he will come to meet us.

'God is looking for us, just as Jesus has made it clear in his parable of the lost sheep.[6] He goes to great lengths to make us aware that we are lost and that he wants to save us. If we allow him, he will accept us as his children and make us heirs of the new earth. That's why I love God.'

'That really sounds good,' Mrs Naumann said in a soft voice.

'Besides a favourite story, I also have a favourite text, a promise I have claimed over and over. It says, "All things work together for good to those who love God."[7] There are very few promises more positive and optimistic than that. And it's why I have to assume that all things which happen to me ultimately work out for good, if I trust God and let him act.'

'You're lucky!'

'Luck has nothing to do with it, because everyone can claim this promise as long as he or she loves God and trusts him. Even if I have fallen flat on my face again, or if something goes terribly wrong in my life, I can always be sure that God will not only help me out of my misery but will even use those negative circumstances to my benefit – even if those negative things do nothing else but contribute to my character development.'

'Whatever doesn't kill you makes you strong, huh?' my co-passenger remarked.

'Something like that, except it comes with the divine guarantee that nothing will kill me – meaning that nothing will rob me of eternal life if I love God and trust him.'

'So you believe that God takes care of us personally?'

'Oh, yes. I and many other Christians have experienced that in a very tangible way. I know that God loves me because Jesus through the Word of God assures me of that love. Sometimes I look around my circle of friends and I almost feel guilty because I am doing much better than they are – despite my many mistakes. Perhaps it is only a subjective impression, but when I review my life I can see so many examples of God's help and love, which make me simply love him more.'

'Sounds as if you have always lived on the sunny side.'

'No, please, no! I have experienced more than my fair share of dark hours,' I conceded. 'Sometimes the problems seemed insurmountable, the dangers huge and the circumstances, humanly speaking, hopeless. Amid that depressing time, I remembered this promise: "All things work together for good to those who love God." After that I calmed down, especially as I remembered how God had helped me in the past.'

'Could you give me an example?'

I thought about it for a while.

'Once, many years ago, I was in a phase of professional reorientation,' I began. 'I had been overseas for several years, and after my return to Germany I had been unemployed, which was not easy for me. In order to have some sort of income, I had a temporary employment agency place me in different industrial companies. At first that was pretty depressing, because in production and warehouses I felt under- and over-challenged at the same time. I was a complete stranger to manufacturing companies because, up to then, I had worked only for charities.

'Years later, looking back, I realised what a good school that work in the manufacturing industry had been for me. When I started to work as a corporate consultant I greatly benefited from my understanding of various industries and industrial and corporate functions. Looking back, I was able to see God's hand in it.

'After that I always said to myself when I got into a difficult situation: "I wonder what ingenious move God will come up with now to turn this situation into a blessing." And, sure enough, it often didn't take long before the Gordian knot was cut before my very eyes. In many cases afterwards I was better off than before.'

'And it always happens that way?' Mrs Naumann asked with an expression of doubt.

'That's what I trust in, as long as I love God. Of course, we do not always find the blessings right away,' I conceded. 'Sometimes it takes years before, by looking back, we can say, "It was good after all that things worked out the way they did," or "God has turned even a defeat into something good. Now I see God's hand in my life. Somehow everything had to be the way it was and worked out for good." '

My neighbour pondered the words for a while. 'That is beautiful.

I can understand what a positive power faith is in your life.'
For a while we just sat there, not saying anything.

Notes:
[1] Luke 24:25, 26, 32, 45-48.
[2] Luke 15:11-17.
[3] Luke 15:17-19.
[4] Luke 15:20.
[5] Luke 15:22-24.
[6] Luke 15:4, 5.
[7] Romans 8:28, NKJV.

CHAPTER TWENTY

A Cheque from Heaven

Walking with God

We had been so steeped in conversation that we hadn't noticed that the sun had risen. The night was over; we hadn't slept, even for a minute.

'You mentioned a few times the concept of experiences with God,' she said, picking up the conversation. 'I still don't understand what you mean by that. Faith for me is something abstract, something not real. But experiences are something tangible. How can I have experiences with Someone whom I can neither see nor hear?'

Her voice, her body language, expressed earnestness, desperation even. I wanted to answer her carefully.

'I experience God in a number of ways,' I said. 'For instance, as a Christian, I frequently read the Bible. In it I find many promises that he gives to us personally.'

'Could you give me an example?'

'The apostle Peter, for instance, invites us to cast all our cares upon him, for he cares for us.[1] In the Bible, God gives us many promises which depend on conditions; for example, to confess our sins,[2] or, as in this case, to really cast our cares or burdens upon God and not continue to drag them around. If I claim his promise, fulfil the conditions, and trust in him, I shall then experience the fact that he really does keep his promises. If that happens once, I can interpret it as coincidence or imagination or whatever. But if it happens over and over again, I see a pattern develop, and that's what I call an experience with God.'

'And what have you experienced in a specific way? I mean, give me a concrete example.'

'OK,' I said. 'Many years ago I was in a difficult financial situation.

In connection with my university studies, I was to go to the United States for six months. But, before my departure, I still needed some money to pay off some debts. That didn't seem like a problem at first, because I had an old car which I wanted to sell. The return would have covered my debts. I already had a buyer. Everything seemed to go well.'

'And then?'

'Then, a few days before the sale of the car, the vehicle needed a new crankshaft. The repair would have cost about 800 Deutschmark (about $400) – money which I didn't have. What was I to do? I needed money for the repair in order to make money through the sale of the car. And time was running out.'

'What happened?'

'At that time I was the guardian of a young man. Years before, a Hamburg court had made me guardian of a young man who had lost both of his parents. As you are aware, it is an honorary responsibility, like jury duty, and so you cannot turn it down. Lothar was 17 years old and lived at a boarding school in Darmstadt near Frankfurt. During his holidays he stayed with me in my Hamburg home. Lothar was not a Christian. On the contrary, he was an avowed Marxist. And yet he politely adapted to the customs of the house and participated in my morning and evening worship.'

'Go on.'

'Well, that evening, on the day I had discovered the damage to my car, I said, "Lothar, I have a problem: I need 800 Deutschmark really fast." I told him the story and suggested, "Why don't we kneel down and pray? God has a thousand ways to help us." '

'What did he do?'

'Interestingly enough, unbelieving Lothar knelt down with me and I asked God to fulfil his promise, which I had just quoted about casting our cares upon him. I left my money problem with God and trusted that somehow he would take care of it.'

'And . . . ?'

'And the next morning I had to go to town, and so Lothar was home alone. When I came back for lunch he was very excited: "The newspaper's just called. They urgently want to talk to you. You must call them back right away. This is the number. They said you are the most-wanted man in town."

'I got scared. What had I done? So I called the paper. "Can you

imagine why we want to talk to you?" the editor asked. "You have just won the poetry award," he said, and asked whether they could come over right away for an interview and the handing over of the cheque." '

'A poetry award? Are you serious?'

'Yes. A few months earlier I had entered a poetry contest in which one had to write a poem about the city of Hamburg, a public relations kind of thing. The contest was sponsored by the city, a bank and that newspaper. Since I had not heard from them for a while, I had just forgotten about it, assuming I hadn't won. But then came this notification – one day after my prayer!'

'How much was the award?'

'It was 2,500, enough to pay for the repairs and then some. Only a few hours later I held a cheque in my hands.'

'That was fantastic.'

'Yes, it was. For me it was not a coincidence, but the fulfilment of God's promise. That was a concrete experience with God. I found especially remarkable the role which unbelieving Lothar played in all this as well.'

'That must have left an enormous impression on him,' Mrs Naumann remarked. 'Did he become a believer after that?'

'Unfortunately not. At least not as long as I knew him. I lost track of him when he reached his eighteenth birthday and my guardianship ended. But many times I asked myself what he might do if in some similar situation.'

She smiled and asked, 'Do you think it always works like that and that everybody else can experience the same thing?'

'Of course, prayer is not a slot machine from which whatever we ask for we get, just as we want and right away, too,' I answered immediately, not wanting to give her the wrong impression. 'And we do not always know what is good for us. Therefore, we should make known to God our wishes and then leave it up to him, trusting in his goodness.'

We were then told to fasten our seatbelts for landing.

'The point is,' I continued, 'that we make one of God's promises the basis for our request, fulfil the named conditions, and trust and obey God.[3] This is important because God cannot bless us if we walk in the wrong direction.'

'That part has become clear to me.'

'In order to experience God, it's important to read the Bible. We do not only get to know God better but we also find out more about his promises and commandments. If we ask for the fulfilment of one of his promises, while trusting and obeying him, he will honour his Word. That's how he demonstrates his trustworthiness and that's how he strengthens our trust in him.'

She remained silent, and so I continued.

'In the course of my life I have experienced many answers to prayer. Not all of them were as spectacular as this, but they were real. All these are, for me, what I mean by experiences with God.'

'This all makes good sense.'

'An important point I don't want to forget, either, is that it is always a threesome: the Word of God, prayer and experience. The Word of God is very important because it helps me interpret my experiences.'

'What do you mean?'

'Well, if I relied only on my personal experiences, impressions or feelings, Satan could easily lead me in the wrong direction. On the other hand, God would not lead me in a way which the Bible describes as dangerous or forbidden. That's how he can correct me through his Word, if I am willing to listen, of course.'

'The Bible, then, helps you understand the experiences?'

'Yes, exactly.'

'Very logical, I think.'

'There is something else I want to say. We can ask God for anything, anything at all. But when I do, I tell myself while I pray that if there is no specific promise which might be the basis for my request, God will answer my prayer the way he sees fit – just as good parents do with their children. I mean, how did you deal with your son's requests? Did you give him whatever he asked for and whenever he wanted it?'

'Certainly not.'

'And in some cases you probably gave your son what he wanted later than he wanted it?'

'Exactly.'

'That's pretty much how God deals with us, as our heavenly Father.[4] Some of our wishes he will grant us right away, some later, some never. Sometimes, we ask for things that are not good for us. If I do not have a specific promise by God as a basis for my request, I add, "Father . . . not my will, but yours, be done." That's how Jesus taught us in the Lord's Prayer.[5] If, on the other hand, I do have a

promise from God, then he has already shown me by that what is his will and what he wants to do for me. Then I can in confidence ask for the fulfilment of that promise and will not add that caveat.'

'That makes sense.'

At that very moment our aircraft touched down on the runway. With a softened rumble below our seats, we touched down. Before reaching the gate, we probably had at least another ten minutes. It was a beautiful sunny morning. I was happy to be back in Frankfurt. Never before had eight hours passed so quickly.

Notes:
[1] 1 Peter 5:7.
[2] 1 John 1:9.
[3] Romans 4:20, 21; 1 John 3:22.
[4] Matthew 7:7-11.
[5] Matthew 6:10.

CHAPTER TWENTY-ONE

Where to from Here?

'You know,' Mrs Naumann said, 'that was a most unusual conversation. Actually, I didn't want to talk about religion. I had long ago given up on it. But many things you said were completely new, interesting and, I must admit, quite convincing. I want to continue thinking about them.'

'I can't ask for more than that.'

'I really would like to find out more about God. But how? I mean, even with all you shared with me, I know so little.'

'If you start reading the New Testament, you will understand many things about Jesus Christ. A modern Bible translation would help too. In every book store you will find a *Good News* version, which has many footnotes and explanations in the appendix.'

'That would seem the best way to begin, wouldn't it?'

'Of course. And I'm offering you two paperbacks by the same author who has helped me understand so much too. One book explains the gospels and what they teach about Jesus, while the other one shows how I can build a relationship with him.'

'You don't have them with you, do you?'

'No, unfortunately not. But I should be happy to send them to you.'

'Would you?'

'I need only your address.'

She took a business card from her handbag and gave it to me. I gave her my card in return. She looked at it for a moment. 'May I call if I have more questions?'

'By all means. And there is something else that might help: a Bible correspondence course based on one of the books I will send you. I will include the respective address so you will know where to get it.'

She seemed very appreciative.

I continued. 'The best thing, of course, would be to join a circle of Christian friends where you could study the Bible together. The denomination I belong to has a church in Düsseldorf. I'll be happy to send you the address.'

'Perhaps that's a bit much for now. First I want to read the books and, perhaps, enrol in the Bible correspondence course.'

After a little pause she added, 'That really was a nice coincidence that we were sitting next to each other.'

'Coincidence?' I said, somewhat exaggeratedly.

She smiled and said, 'Maybe not.'

'You know, Mrs Naumann, before leaving, I had prayed and asked for four seats so I could stretch out and sleep. But then I quickly realised that that was a pretty selfish request. So I continued my prayer, "If, however, there will be a person on the plane who would like to find out about you, then, please, let me sit next to that person."

'I believe the two of us had a divine appointment last night. That was no coincidence but an experience with God.'

'I can understand why you are saying that,' Mrs Naumann said. 'I believe last night I got quite a bit closer to him.'

Our goodbye was brief and cordial.

I'm convinced, too, that it won't be forever.